Published in January 2012 in Great Britain
by Juju Vail and Susan Cropper, Loop
Copyright Juju Vail and Susan Cropper, Loop
15 Camden Passage, Islington
London N1 8EA
www.loopknitting.com

ISBN:9780957012806
A CIP catalogue record for this book is available
from the British Library
Printed in Spain by Graficas Cems

contents

old maiden aunt yarns, hand~dyed in scotland
~ we love knitting with hand~dyed yarns
for their richness and depth of colour as well as
their uniqueness. they are little gems that
add a touch of the personal and handmade.

cedar shake fingerless gloves

This pattern has it all ~ lace, twisted stitches and ribbing. It stretches and contracts beautifully to give a well ~ fitted fingerless mitten with wrist ~ narrowing appeal while the wavy lines work to elongate the arm. It looks best in subtle semi ~ solid, hand ~ paint yarns such as luxurious madelinetosh Pashmina or Handmaiden Casbah.

Yarn:
madelinetosh Pashmina: 75% superwash wool, 15% silk and 10% cashmere, 100g = 329m/360yd, 1 skein
Colour shown: Celadon (see page 13)

Handmaiden Casbah: 81% superwash merino, 10% nylon, 9% cashmere, 115g = 325m/355 yd, 1 skein
Colour shown: Topaz (see opposite)

Any sportweight yarn should work; look for one in a solid or semi-solid colour with a little sheen from silk or very tightly twisted wool.

Gauge: 10cm/4in = 26sts in stocking stitch

Needles: 3mm/US 3 dpns or 100cm/40in circular needle if using 'magic loop' technique

Notions: stitch markers, scrap yarn, darning needle

Pattern (make two):
Cast on 60sts and join in the round, being careful not to twist the stitches. Place a marker to signify beginning of round. Follow Cedar Shake Chart A or Written Instructions, repeating the 12sts a total of 5 times and the chart a total of 3 times (36 rounds total).

Cedar Shake Chart A

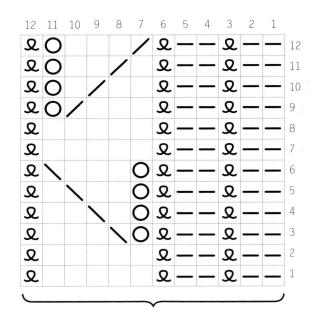

Repeat five times

these cedar shakes are knit with
handmaiden 'casbah' in topaz and,
on page thirteen, knit with
madelinetosh 'pashmina' in celadon

Cedar Shake Chart A (see previous page)

Cedar Shake A Written instructions
Round 1: *P2, ktbl, p2, ktbl, k5, ktbl*, rep * to * four more times.
Round 2: *P2, ktbl, p2, ktbl, k5, ktbl*, rep * to * four more times.
Round 3: *P2, ktbl, p2, ktbl, yo, ssk, k3, ktbl*, rep * to * four more times.
Round 4: *P2, ktbl, p2, ktbl, yo, k1, ssk, k2, ktbl*, rep * to * four more times.
Round 5: *P2, ktbl, p2, ktbl, yo, k2, ssk, k1, ktbl*, rep * to * four more times.
Round 6: *P2, ktbl, p2, ktbl, yo, k3, ssk, ktbl*, rep * to * four more times.
Round 7: *P2, ktbl, p2, ktbl, k5, ktbl*, rep * to * four more times.
Round 8: *P2, ktbl, p2, ktbl, k5, ktbl*, rep * to * four more times.
Round 9: *P2, ktbl, p2, ktbl, k3, k2tog, yo, ktbl*, rep * to * four more times.
Round 10: *P2, ktbl, p2, ktbl, k2, k2tog, k1, yo, ktbl*, rep * to * four more times.
Round 11: *P2, ktbl, p2, ktbl, k1, k2tog, k2, yo, ktbl*, rep * to * four more times.
Round 12: *P2, ktbl, p2, ktbl, k2tog, k3, yo, ktbl*, rep * to * four more times.

Now work Cedar Shake Chart B or Written Instructions, Decrease Round.
Then work Rounds 1 – 12 twice. (You will have now worked a total of 61 rounds.) On the last round 12, place another marker to signify thumb gusset as follows: slm, work 3sts, pm, continue the round in pattern until you come to the first marker.

Cedar Shake Chart B (see left)

Cedar Shake B Written Instructions
Decrease Round: *P2tog, ktbl, p2tog, ktbl, k5, ktbl*, rep * to * four more times. 50sts

Round 1: * P1, ktbl, p1, ktbl, k5, ktbl*, rep * to * four more times.
Round 2: *P1, ktbl, p1, ktbl, yo, ssk, k3, ktbl*, rep * to * four more times.
Round 3: *P1, ktbl, p1, ktbl, yo, k1, ssk, k2, ktbl*, rep * to * four more times.
Round 4: *P1, ktbl, p1, ktbl, yo, k2, ssk, k1, ktbl*, rep * to * four more times.
Round 5: *P1, ktbl, p1, ktbl, yo, k3, ssk, ktbl*, rep * to * four more times.
Round 6: *P1, ktbl, p1, ktbl, k5, ktbl*, rep * to * four more times.
Round 7: *P1, ktbl, p1, ktbl, k5, ktbl*, rep * to * four more times.
Round 8: *P1, ktbl, p1, ktbl, k3, k2tog, yo, ktbl*, rep * to * four more times.
Round 9: *P1, ktbl, p1, ktbl, k2, k2tog, k1, yo, ktbl*, rep * to * four more times.
Round 10: *P1, ktbl, p1, ktbl, k1, k2tog, k2, yo, ktbl*, rep * to * four more times.
Round 11: *P1, ktbl, p1, ktbl, k2tog, k3, yo, ktbl*, rep * to * four more times.
Round 12: *P1, ktbl, p1, ktbl, k5, ktbl*, rep * to * four more times.

Thumb Gusset Shaping
Work the thumb gusset pattern between markers. Begin by slipping the first marker, rli, p1, ktbl, p1, lli, slip marker, and then continue with the rest of the Cedar Shake pattern (stitches 14-20 on thumb gusset chart). Continue to repeat the Cedar Shake

Cedar Shake Chart B

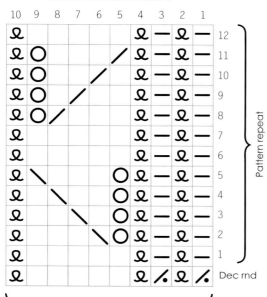

Pattern repeat

Dec rnd

Repeat five times
(Four times while working thumb gusset chart)

Thumb Gusset Chart

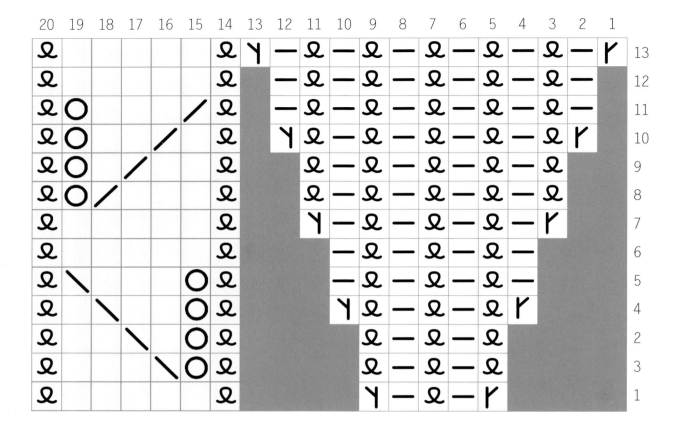

B pattern over the rest of the stitches. Between markers, follow the thumb gusset shaping from the chart or written instructions and work the Cedar Shake B pattern over the rest of the stitches.

Thumb Gusset Chart (see above)

Thumb Gusset Written Instructions
These are written instructions for the entire mitt circumference, including the thumb gusset area.

Round 1: Rli, p1, ktbl, p1, lli, ktbl, k5, ktbl, *p1, ktbl, p1, ktbl, k5, ktbl*, rep * to * three more times.
Round 2: Ktbl, p1, ktbl, p1, ktbl twice, yo, ssk, k3, ktbl, *p1, ktbl, p1, ktbl, yo, ssk, k3, ktbl*, rep * to * three more times.
Round 3: Ktbl, p1, ktbl, p1, ktbl twice, yo, k1, ssk, k2, ktbl, *p1, ktbl, p1, ktbl, yo, k1, ssk, k2, ktbl*, rep * to * three more times.
Round 4: Rli, ktbl, p1, ktbl, p1, ktbl, lli, ktbl, yo, k2, ssk, k1, ktbl, *p1, ktbl, p1, ktbl, yo, k2, ssk, k1, ktbl*, rep * to * three more times.
Round 5: P1, ktbl, p1, ktbl, p1, ktbl, p1, ktbl, yo, k3, ssk, ktbl, *p1, ktbl, p1, ktbl, yo, k3, ssk, ktbl*, rep * to * three more times.
Round 6: P1, ktbl, p1, ktbl, p1, ktbl, p1, ktbl, k5, ktbl, *p1, ktbl, p1, ktbl, k5, ktbl*, rep * to * three more times.
Round 7: Rli, p1, ktbl, p1, ktbl, p1, ktbl, p1, lli, ktbl, k5,

ktbl, *p1, ktbl, p1, ktbl, k5, ktbl*, rep * to * three more times.
Round 8: Ktbl, p1, ktbl, p1, ktbl, p1, ktbl, p1, ktbl twice, k3, k2tog, yo, ktbl, *p1, ktbl, p1, ktbl, k3, k2tog, yo, ktbl*, rep * to * three more times.
Round 9: Ktbl, p1, ktbl, p1, ktbl, p1, ktbl, p1, ktbl twice, k2, k2tog, k1, yo, ktbl, *p1, ktbl, p1, ktbl, k2, k2tog, k1, yo, ktbl*, rep * to * three more times.
Round 10: Rli, ktbl, p1, ktbl, p1, ktbl, p1, ktbl, p1, ktbl, lli, ktbl, k1, k2tog, k2, yo, ktbl, *p1, ktbl, p1, ktbl, k1, k2tog, k2, yo, ktbl*, rep * to * three more times.
Round 11: P1, ktbl, p1, ktbl, p1, ktbl, p1, ktbl, p1, ktbl, p1, ktbl, k2tog, k3, yo, ktbl, *p1, ktbl, p1, ktbl, k2tog, k3, yo, ktbl*, rep * to * three more times.
Round 12: P1, ktbl, p1, ktbl, p1, ktbl, p1, ktbl, p1, ktbl, p1, ktbl, k5, ktbl, *p1, ktbl, p1, ktbl, k5, ktbl*, rep * to * three more times.
Round 13: Rli, p1, ktbl, p1, ktbl, p1, ktbl, p1, ktbl, p1, ktbl, p1, lli, ktbl, k5, ktbl, *p1, ktbl, p1, ktbl, k5, ktbl*, rep * to * three more times.

Remove marker and place the 13 thumb gusset stitches on a length of scrap yarn. Cast on 3sts using the 'backward loop' method. Remove the second marker and continue knitting around the mitt following Cedar Shake B, rounds 2-12, starting at stitch 4. Repeat rounds 1-7. Repeat Round 7 once more for a total of 18 rounds from the thumb.

Braided Edge
You will need an extra length of the same yarn to create the braided edge; either use the other end of the ball or cut a 3m/3yd length. Leaving a 15cm/6in tail to weave in later, bring both yarns to the front of the work, and continue as follows:
Round 1: *P1 with one strand and then p1 with the other, always bringing the next strand to be used over the top of the last*, rep * to * for entire round.
Round 2: *P1 with one strand and then p1 with the other, always bringing the next strand to be used under the last*, rep * to * for entire round.
Cast off knitwise.

Thumb
Pick up all 13sts held on scrap yarn. Then join yarn and pick up 5sts from the cast on edge of palm. Knit the 18 thumb stitches in 9 repeats of the thumb rib pattern for 10 rounds. Cast off knitwise.

Thumb Rib Chart (see above, right)

Thumb Rib Chart

2 1

Thumb Rib Written Instructions
Ktbl, p1, rep * to * 8 more times.

Weave in ends.

prairie shawl knit in dyeforyarn
'merino & mulberry silk fingering' in
antique doll

knitting nupps

nupps are the delicate bobbles
often found in traditional estonian
lace shawls

prairie shawl

It's tempting to write a book full of shawl patterns. They're our favourite knitted item – fun to make and great to wear. We like them wrapped over our shoulders, either unfastened or closed with a pin. We designed the Prairie Shawl with a shoulder hug in mind and a lust for nupps. The upper edge curves slightly so that it's cosy when it sits around shoulders; making it in a fingering weight yarn will give good coverage, while a fine lace yarn will make the perfect size neck wrap.

Size:
Laceweight version – approx. 104cm/41in wide, 48cm/19in deep
4ply/fingering version – approx. 130cm/51in wide, 58cm/23in deep

Yarn:
This shawl can be made in any lace or 4ply/fingering weight yarn.

Laceweight versions:
madelinetosh Prairie: 100% superwash merino wool, 100g = 768m/840yd, 1 skein
Colour shown: Fragrant (just seen on page 98)

Malabrigo Yarn Lace: 100% baby merino wool, 50g = 430m/470yd, 2 skeins
Colour shown: Frank Ochre(see previous page)

4ply/fingering weight version:
DyeForYarn Fingering Merino & Silk: 75% superwash merino, 25% mulberry silk, 100g = 400m/437yd, 2 skeins
Colour shown: Antique Doll (see page 14)

Gauge: Your gauge is not crucial in this pattern but you may use the following information as a guide.
Laceweight version: 10cm/4in = approx. 24sts in stocking stitch
4ply/fingering weight version: 10cm/4in = approx. 22sts in stocking stitch

Needles:
Circular 'lace' needles, with their pointier tips, are strongly recommended for this pattern. Make sure you have a circular needle for working the lace trim of at

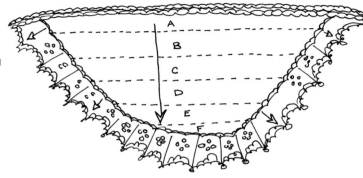

diagram of construction

least 100cm/40in length. The shawl body can be worked on the same circular needle or with straight needles.

Laceweight version in Prairie or Malabrigo Yarn Lace: 3.25mm/US 3
Fingering weight version in DyeForYarn: 3.5mm/US 4

Notions: stitch markers, darning needle, stitch holder

Note:
There are three edge stitches on each side. These are always knit, with the first one in each row slipped purlwise with the yarn in front. Begin each row with s1wyif, k2, and end each row with k3.

To create a row of eyelet holes along the cast on edge, as in our Malabrigo version, knit one row of yo, k2tog instead of a plain row of knit for the fourth row after cast on.

Instructions:
CO 246sts. Knit 5 rows, slipping the first stitch of every row with yarn in front. On the 6th row, s1wyif, k2, pm, *k16, pm*, rep * to * fourteen times, k3.

Begin Prairie Lace pattern, using Chart A or written instructions, and then continue with Charts B through F.

Chart A (see right)

Written Instructions for Chart A
Row 1 (RS): S1wyif, k2, k9, yo, k1, yo, k3, sk2p, *k9, yo,

nupp 7
In this pattern we use the simplest method of working nupps: very loosely working (k1, yo, k1, yo, k1, yo, k1) all in the same stitch, and then purling these 7 new stitches together on the following row.

Here is another method of working nupps that you may find works better for you:

Working very loosely, work (k1, yo, k1, yo, k1, yo, k1) all in the same stitch - 7 nupp sts made from 1st. Turn the work before continuing with the row and knit together or purl together through the back of the 7 nupp stitches.

This will prevent them from tightening up. Purl or knit as usual, in the next row.

Chart A

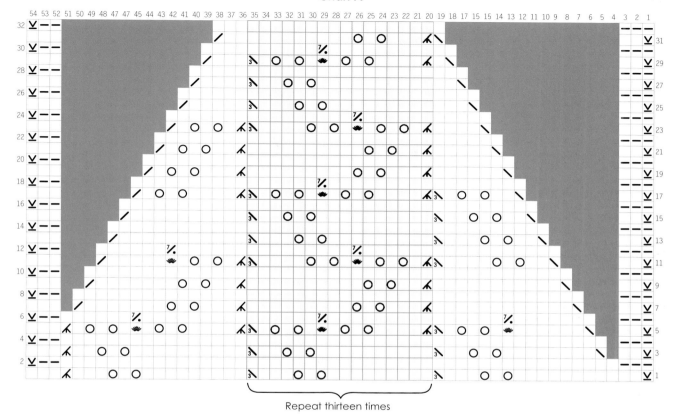

Repeat thirteen times

k1, yo, k3, sk2p*, rep * to * twelve more times, k9, yo, k1, yo, k3, k3tog, k3. 246sts

Row 2 and all other WS rows for Chart A: S1wyif, k2, purl all stitches until last 3, k3. If there was a nupp in the previous row, decrease it to one stitch by p7tog the stitches created by nupp7.

Row 3: S1wyif, k2, ssk, k8, yo, k1, yo, k2, sk2p, *k10, yo, k1, yo, k2, sk2p*, rep * to * twelve more times, k10, yo, k1, yo, k2, k3tog, k3. 245sts

Row 5: S1wyif, k2, ssk, k6, nupp7, k1, yo, k1, yo, k1, sk2p, *k3tog, k4, yo, k1, yo, k1, nupp7, k1, yo, k1, yo, k1, sk2p*, rep * to * twelve more times, k3tog, k4, yo, k1, yo, k1, nupp7, k1, yo, k1, yo, k1, k3tog, k3. 244sts

Row 7: S1wyif, k2, ssk, k12, *k3tog, k3, yo, k1, yo, k9*, rep * to * twelve more times, k3tog, k3, yo, k1, yo, k7, k2tog, k3. 242sts

Row 9: S1wyif, k2, ssk, k11, *k3tog, k2, yo, k1, yo, k10*, rep * to * twelve more times, k3tog, k2, yo, k1, yo, k7, k2tog, k3. 240sts

Row 11: S1wyif, k2, ssk, k2, yo, k1, yo, k4, sk2p, *k3tog, k1, yo, k1, yo, k1, nupp7, k1, yo, k1, yo, k4, sk2p*, rep * to * twelve more times, k3tog, k1, yo, k1, yo, k1, nupp7, k5, k2tog, k3. 238sts

Row 13: S1wyif, k2, ssk, k2, yo, k1, yo, k3, sk2p, *k9, yo, k1, yo, k3, sk2p*, rep * to * twelve more times, k11, k2tog, k3. 236sts

Row 15: S1wyif, k2, ssk, k2, yo, k1, yo, k2, sk2p, *k10, yo, k1, yo, k2, sk2p*, rep * to * twelve more times, k10, k2tog, k3. 234sts

Row 17: S1wyif, k2, ssk, k2, yo, k1, yo, k1, sk2p, *k3tog, k4, yo, k1, yo, k1, nupp7, k1, yo, k1, yo, k1, sk2p*, rep * to * twelve more times, k3tog, k4, yo, k1, yo, k1, k2tog, k3. 232sts

Row 19: S1wyif, k2, ssk, k6, *k3tog, k3, yo, k1, yo, k9*, rep

* to * twelve more times, k3tog, k3, yo, k1, yo, k1, k2tog, k3. 230sts

Row 21: S1wyif, k2, ssk, k5, *k3tog, k2, yo, k1, yo, k10*, rep * to * twelve more times, k3tog, k2, yo, k1, yo, k1, k2tog, k3. 228sts

Row 23: S1wyif, k2, ssk, k4, *k3tog, k1, yo, k1, yo, k1, nupp7, k1, yo, k1, yo, k4, sk2p*, rep * to * twelve more times, k3tog, k1, yo, k1, yo, k1, k2tog, k3. 226sts

Row 25: S1wyif, k2, ssk, k3, *k9, yo, k1, yo, k3, sk2p*, rep * to * twelve more times, k5, k2tog, k3. 224sts

Row 27: S1wyif, k2, ssk, k2, *k10, yo, k1, yo, k2, sk2p*, rep * to * twelve more times, k4, k2tog, k3. 222sts

Row 29: S1wyif, k2, ssk, k1, *k3tog, k4, yo, k1, yo, k1, nupp7, k1, yo, k1, yo, k1, sk2p*, rep * to * twelve more times, k3, k2tog, k3. 220sts

Row 31: S1wyif, k2, ssk, *k3tog, k3, yo, k1, yo, k9*, rep * to * twelve more times, k2, k2tog, k3. 218sts

Row 32: S1wyif, k2, purl all stitches until last 3, k3. 218sts

Written Instructions for Chart B

Row 33: S1wyif, k2, ssk, k15, *k3tog, k2, yo, k1, yo, k10*, rep * to * ten more times, k3tog, k2, yo, k1, yo, k11, k2tog, k3. 216sts

Row 34 and all other WS rows: S1wyif, k2, purl all stitches until last 3, k3. If there was a nupp in the previous row,decrease it to one stitch by p7tog the stitches created by nupp7.

Row 35: S1wyif, k2, ssk, k4, nupp7, k1, yo, k1, yo, k4, sk2p, *k3tog, k1, yo, k1, yo, k1, nupp7, k1, yo, k1, yo, k4, sk2p*, rep * to * ten more times, k3tog, k1, yo, k1, yo, k1, nupp7, k9, k2tog, k3. 214sts

Row 37: S1wyif, k2, ssk, k6, yo, k1, yo, k3, s1 k2tog psso, *k9, yo, k1, yo, k3, sk2p*, rep * to * ten more times, k15, k2tog, k3. 212sts

Row 39: S1wyif, k2, ssk, k6, yo, k1, yo, k3, sk2p, *k10, yo, k1, yo, k2, sk2p*, rep * to * ten more times, k14, k2tog, k3. 210sts

Row 41: S1wyif, k2, ssk, k4, nupp7, k1, yo, k1, yo, k1, sk2p, *k3tog, k4, yo, k1, yo, k1, nupp7, k1, yo, k1, yo, k1,

Chart B

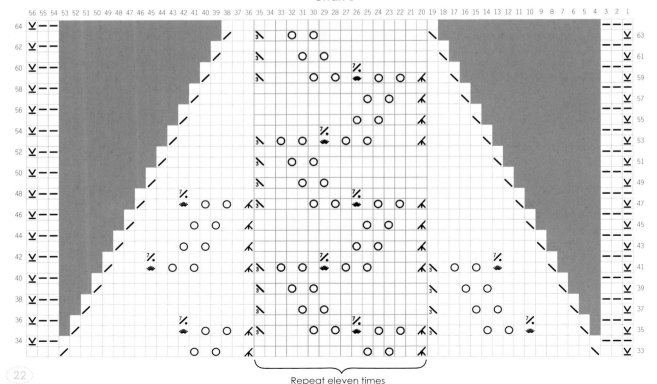

Repeat eleven times

sk2p*, rep * to * ten more times, k3tog, k4, yo, k1, yo, k1, nupp7, k3, k2tog, k3. 208sts
Row 43: S1wyif, k2, ssk, k10, *k3tog, k3, yo, k1, yo, k9*, rep * to * ten more times, k3tog, k3, yo, k1, yo, k5, k2tog, k3. 206sts
Row 45: S1wyif, k2, ssk, k9, *k3tog, k2, yo, k1, yo, k10*, rep * to * ten more times, k3tog, k2, yo, k1, yo, k5, k2tog, k3. 204sts
Row 47: S1wyif, k2, ssk, k8, *k3tog, k1, yo, k1, yo, k1, nupp7, k1, yo, k1, yo, k4, sk2p*, rep * to * ten more times, k3tog, k1, yo, k1, yo, k1, nupp7, k3, k2tog, k3. 202sts
Row 49: S1wyif, k2, ssk, k7, *k9, yo, k1, yo, k3, sk2p*, rep * to * ten more times, k9, k2tog, k3. 200sts
Row 51: S1wyif, k2, ssk, k6, *k10, yo, k1, yo, k2, sk2p*, rep * to * ten more times, k8, k2tog, k3. 198sts
Row 53: S1wyif, k2, ssk, k5, *k3tog, k4, yo, k1, yo, k1, nupp7, k1, yo, k1, yo, k1, sk2p*, rep * to * ten more times, k7, k2tog, k3. 196sts
Row 55: S1wyif, k2, ssk, k4, *k3tog, k3, yo, k1, yo, k9*, rep * to * ten more times, k6, k2tog, k3. 194sts
Row 57: S1wyif, k2, ssk, k3, *k3tog, k2, yo, k1, yo, k10*, rep * to * ten more times, k5, k2tog, k3. 192 sts
Rw 59: S1wyif, k2, ssk, k2, *k3tog, k1, yo, k1, yo, k1, nupp7, k1, yo, k1, yo, k4, sk2p*, rep * to * ten more times, k4, k2tog, k3. 190sts
Row 61: S1wyif, k2, ssk, k1, *k9, yo, k1, yo, k3, sk2p*, rep * to * ten more times, k3, k2tog, k3. 188sts
Row 63: S1wyif, k2, ssk, *k10, yo, k1, yo, k2, sk2p*, rep * to * ten more times, k2, k2tog, k3. 186sts
Row 64: S1wyif, k2, purl all stitches until last 3, k3. 186sts

Decreasing will now occur on both the RS and WS; 4sts are decreased every two rows.

Chart C (see below)

Written instructions for Chart C
Row 65: S1wyif, k2, ssk, k8, nupp7, k1, yo, k1, yo, k1, sk2p, *k3tog, k4, yo, k1, yo, k1, nupp7, k1, yo, k1, yo, k1, sk2p*, rep * to * eight more times, k3tog, k4, yo, k1, yo, k1, nupp7, k1, yo, k1, yo, k1, sk2p, k1, k2tog, k3. 184sts
Row 66 and all other WS rows: S1wyif, k2, p2tog, purl to last 5sts, p2tog tbl, k3. If there was a nupp in the previous row, decrease it to one stitch by p7tog the stitches created by nupp7.
Row 67: S1wyif, k2, ssk, k13, *k3tog, k3, yo, k1, yo, k9*, rep * to * eight more times, k3tog, k3, yo, k1, yo, k8, k2tog, k3. 180sts
Row 69: S1wyif, k2, ssk, k11, *k3tog, k2, yo, k1, yo, k10*, rep * to * eight more times, k3tog, k2, yo, k1, yo, k7, k2tog, k3. 176sts
Row 71: S1wyif, k2, ssk, k9, *k3tog, k1, yo, k1, yo, k1, nupp7, k1, yo, k1, yo, k4, sk2p*, rep * to * eight more times, k3tog, k1, yo, k1, yo, k1, nupp7, k4, k2tog, k3. 172sts
Row 73: S1wyif, k2, ssk, k7, *k9, yo, k1, yo, k3, sk2p*, rep * to * eight more times, k9, k2tog, k3. 168sts
Row 75: S1wyif, k2, ssk, k5, *k10, yo, k1, yo, k2, sk2p*, rep * to * eight more times, k7, k2tog, k3. 164sts
Row 77: S1wyif, k2, ssk, k3, *k3tog, k4, yo, k1, yo, k1,

On charts C, D, E and F decreasing occurs on both the right and wrong sides of fabric; 4 stitches are decreased every two rows.

Chart C

Repeat nine times

Chart D

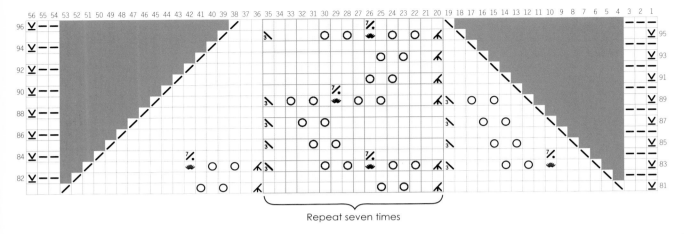

Repeat seven times

Chart E

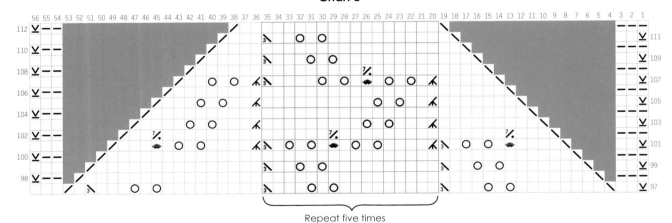

Repeat five times

nupp7, k1, yo, k1, yo, k1, sk2p*, rep * to * eight more times, k5, k2tog, k3. 160sts
Row 79: S1wyif, k2, ssk, k1, *k3tog, k3, yo, k1, yo, k9*, rep * to * eight more times, k3, k2tog, k3. 156sts
Row 80: S1wyif, k2, p2tog, purl to last 5sts, p2tog tbl, k3. 154sts

Chart D (see above)

Written Instructions for Chart D
Row 81: S1wyif, k2, ssk, k15, *k3tog, k2, yo, k1, yo, k10*, rep * to * six more times, k3tog, k2, yo, k1, yo, k11,

k2tog, k3. 152sts
Row 82 and all other WS rows: S1wyif, k2, p2tog, purl to last 5sts, p2tog tbl, k3. If there was a nupp in the previous row, decrease it to one stitch by p7tog the stitches created by nupp7.
Row 83: S1wyif, k2, ssk, k3, nupp7, k1, yo, k1, yo, k4,sk2p, *k3tog, k1, yo, k1, yo, k1, nupp7, k1, yo, k1, yo, k4, sk2p*, rep * to * six more times, k3tog, k1, yo, k1, yo, k1, nupp7, k8, k2tog, k3. 148sts
Row 85: S1wyif, k2, ssk, k4, yo, k1, yo, k3, sk2p, *k9, yo, k1, yo, k3, sk2p*, rep * to * six more times, k13, k2tog, k3. 144sts

Chart F

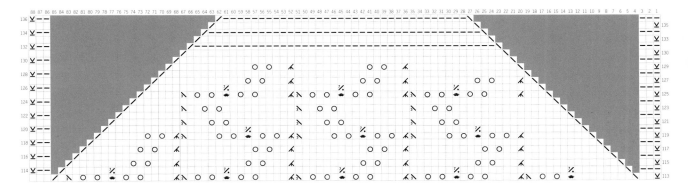

Row 87: S1wyif, k2, ssk, k3, yo, k1, yo, k2, sk2p, *k10, yo, k1, yo, k2, sk2p*, rep * to * six more times, k11, k2tog, k3. 140sts

Row 89: S1wyif, k2, ssk, k2, yo, k1, yo, k1, sk2p, *k3tog, k4, yo, k1, yo, k1, nupp7, k1, yo, k1, yo, k1, sk2p*, rep * to * six more times, k9, k2tog, k3. 136sts

Row 91: S1wyif, k2, ssk, k5, *k3tog, k3, yo, k1, yo, k9*, rep * to * six more times, k7, k2tog, k3. 132sts

Row 93: S1wyif, k2, ssk, k3, *k3tog, k2, yo, k1, yo, k10*, rep * to * six more times, k5, k2tog, k3. 128sts

Row 95: S1wyif, k2, ssk, k1, *k3tog, k1, yo, k1, yo, k1, nupp7, k1, yo, k1, yo, k4, sk2p*, rep * to * six more times, k3, k2tog, k3. 124sts

Row 96: S1wyif, k2, p2tog, purl to last 5sts, p2tog tbl, k3. 122sts

Chart E (see opposite)

Written Instructions for Chart E

Row 97: S1wyif, k2, ssk, k8, yo, k1, yo, k3, sk2p, *k9, yo, k1, yo, k3, sk2p*, rep * to * four more times, k9, yo, k1, yo, k3, sk2p, k1, k2tog, k3. 120sts

Row 98 and all other WS rows: S1wyif, k2, p2tog, purl to last 5sts, p2tog tbl, k3. If there was a nupp in the previous row, decrease it to one stitch by p7tog the stitches created by nupp7.

Row 99: S1wyif, k2, ssk, k7, yo, k1, yo, k2, sk2p, *k10, yo, k1, yo, k2, sk2p*, rep * to * four more times, k15, k2tog, k3. 116sts

Row 101: S1wyif, k2, ssk, k4, nupp7, k1, yo, k1, yo, k1, sk2p, *k3tog, k4, yo, k1, yo, k1, nupp7, k1, yo, k1, yo, k1, sk2p*, rep * to * four more times, k3tog, k4, yo, k1, yo, k1, nupp7, k3, k2tog, k3. 112sts

Row 103: S1wyif, k2, ssk, k9, *k3tog, k3, yo, k1, yo, k9*, rep * to * four more times, k3tog, k3, yo, k1, yo, k4, k2tog, k3. 108sts

Row 105: S1wyif, k2, ssk, k7, *k3tog, k2, yo, k1, yo, k10*, rep * to * four more times, k3tog, k2, yo, k1, yo, k3, k2tog, k3. 104sts

Row 107: S1wyif, k2, ssk, k5, *k3tog, k1, yo, k1, yo, k1, nupp7, k1, yo, k1, yo, k4, sk2p*, rep * to * four more times, k3tog, k1, yo, k1, yo, k2, k2tog, k3. 100sts

Row 109: S1wyif, k2, ssk, k3, *k9, yo, k1, yo, k3, sk2p*, rep * to * four more times, k5, k2tog, k3. 96sts

Row 111: S1wyif, k2, ssk, k1, *k10, yo, k1, yo, k2, sk2p*, rep * to * four more times, k3, k2tog, k3. 92sts

Row 112: S1wyif, k2, p2tog, purl to last 5sts, k3. 90sts

Chart F (see above)

Written Instructions for Chart F

Row 113: S1wyif, k2, ssk, k8, nupp7, k1, yo, k1, yo, k1, sk2p, *k3tog, k4, yo, k1, yo, k1, nupp7, k1, yo, k1, yo, k1, sk2p*, rep * to * two more times, k3tog, k4, yo, k1, yo, k1, nupp7, k1, yo, k1, yo, k1, sk2p, k1, k2tog, k3. 88sts

Row 114 and all other WS rows: S1wyif, k2, p2tog, purl to last 5sts, p2tog tbl, k3. If there was a nupp in the previous row, decrease it to one stitch by p7tog the stitches created by nupp7.

Row 115: S1wyif, k2, ssk, k13, *k3tog, k3, yo, k1, yo, k9*, rep * to * two more times, k3tog, k3, yo, k1, yo, k8, k2tog, k3. 84sts

Row 117: S1wyif, k2, ssk, k11, *k3tog, k2, yo, k1, yo, k10*, rep * to * two more times, k3tog, k2, yo, k1, yo, k7, k2tog, k3. 80sts

Row 119: S1wyif, k2, ssk, k9, *k3tog, k1, yo, k1, yo, k1, nupp7, k1, yo, k1, yo, k4, sk2p*, rep * to * two more times, k3tog, k1, yo, k1, yo, k6, k2tog, k3. 76sts

Row 121: S1wyif, k2, ssk, k7, *k9, yo, k1, yo, k3, sk2p*, rep * to * two more times, k9, k2tog, k3. 72sts
Row 123: S1wyif, k2, ssk, k5, *k10, yo, k1, yo, k2, sk2p*, rep * to * two more times, k7, k2tog, k3. 68sts
Row 125: S1wyif, k2, ssk, k3, *k3tog, k4, yo, k1, yo, k1, nupp7, k1, yo, k1, yo, k1, sk2p*, rep * to * two more times, k5, k2tog, k3. 64sts
Row 127: S1wyif, k2, ssk, k1, *k3tog, k3, yo, k1, yo, k9*, rep * to * two more times, k3, k2tog, k3. 60sts
Row 129: S1wyif, k2, k15, *k3tog, k2, yo, k1, yo, k10*, rep * to * once more, k1, k2tog, k3. 56sts
Row 131(RS): S1wyif, k2, ssk, knit to last 5sts, k2tog, k3. 52sts
Row 132 (WS): S1wyif, k2, ssk, k42, k2tog, k3. 50sts
Row 133: S1wyif, k2, ssk, k40, k2tog, k3. 48sts
Row 134: S1wyif, k2, ssk, k38, k2tog, k3. 46sts
Row 135: S1wyif, k2, ssk, k36, k2tog, k3. 44sts
Row 136: S1wyif, k2, ssk, k34, k2tog, k3. 42sts

Transfer 42sts to stitch holder.

Lace Edging
The lace edging is knit by picking up stitches from the long, curved edge of the shawl. The bottom edge is gathered slightly by picking up extra stitches around corners and at the bottom.

Before beginning to pick up stitches, place markers to help with correct stitch pick up. With the RS of shawl facing, place markers 5 edge stitches from either side of the two bottom corners.

With RS facing, starting at the upper left corner, pick up and knit 72sts along left side edge, up until the first marker. Pick up through the front and backs of stitches to increase pick up rate around corner, so that you have picked up 20sts in the 10sts before the next marker (five of these will be 'held' stitches).
Pick up and knit 40sts into the next 32sts held at the bottom edge of shawl, before the next marker.

Double pick up again (through fronts and backs of stitches), so that you pick up another 20sts before the next marker. Pick up and knit 73sts along right edge before the top right corner; 225sts. Knit one row.

Work the first four stitches according to the chart or written instructions. Knit the lace repeat (highlighted repeat on chart) a total of twenty-one times. Knit the last 11sts following the chart or written instructions (stitches 18-28 on chart).

Follow the nineteen rows of chart or written instructions.

Lace Edge Chart (see left)

Lace Edge Written Instructions
Row 1 (RS): K2, ssk, yo, *k7, yo, cdd, yo*, rep * to * twenty more times, k7, yo, k2tog, k2. 225sts
Row 2: K2, p221, k2.
Row 3: K2, ssk, yo, *k3, nupp7, k3, yo, cdd, yo*, rep * to * twenty more times, k3, nupp7, k3, yo, k2tog, k2.
Row 4: K2, p2, *p3, p7tog, p6*, rep * to * twenty more times, p3, p7tog, p5, k2.
Row 5: K2, ssk, yo, *k2, nupp7, k1, nupp7, k2, yo, cdd, yo*, rep * to * twenty more times, k2, nupp7, k1, nupp7, k2, yo, k2tog, k2.

Lace Edge Chart

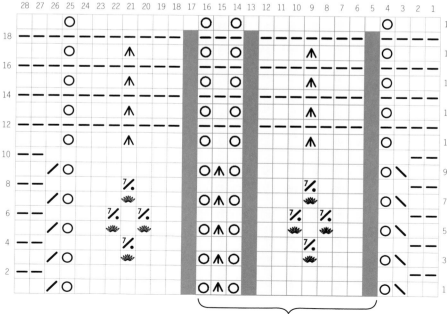

Repeat twenty-one times

Row 6: K2, p2, *p2, p7tog, p1, p7tog, p5*, rep * to * twenty more times, p2, p7tog, p1, p7tog, p4, k2.

Row 7: K2, ssk, yo, *k3, nupp7, k3, yo, cdd, yo*, rep to * twenty more times, k3, nupp7, k3, yo, k2tog, k2.

Row 8: K2, p2, *p3, p7tog, p6*, rep * to * twenty more times, p3, p7tog, p5, k2.

Row 9: K2, ssk, yo, *k7, yo, cdd, yo*, rep * to * twenty more times, k7, yo, k2tog, k2.

Row 10: k2, p221, k2.

Rows 11, 13, 15 & 17: K3, yo, *k3, cdd, k3, yo, k1, yo*, rep * to * twenty more times, k3, cdd, k3, yo, k3.

Rows 12, 14, 16 & 18: K225.

Row 19: K3, yo, *k9, yo, k1, yo*, rep * to * twenty more times, k8, yo, k3. 267sts

Cast off loosely: K2, *sl2 back to left needle, k2tog tbl, k1*, rep * to * to end of row.

Weave in ends and wet block with T-pins and blocking wires.

oak knot hat

The opening and closing of cables in this pattern reminds us of the knots in a beautifully grained piece of wood and we think it works up great for men or women. The twisted stitches in this hat only cross as a two-stitch cable occasionally, making it a very easy pattern to work, especially as you don't need a cable needle.

Size:
One size fits most. Hat is designed with negative ease to stretch over head.
Height from brim to crown: 21cm/8.25in
Un-stretched width around brim: 42cm/16.5in

Yarn:
Juno Pearl: 40% superfine alpaca, 40% merino and 20% silk, 100g = 230m/251yd, 1 skein
Colour shown: Bittersweet (see opposite)

Gauge:
10cm/4in = 25sts x 34 rows in Oak Knot Twist pattern, washed and measured lying flat, un-stretched.

Needles:
2.5mm/US 2, 40cm/16in circular needle for brim ribbing
3mm/US 3 circular needle for body of hat: You can use a 100cm/40in circular needle, using the 'magic loop' technique for the entire body of the hat, or use a 40cm/16in circular needle for the hat and a set of dpns for the crown decreases.

Notions: stitch marker, darning needle

Pattern:
CO 132sts with smaller needles. Join to work in the round, being careful not to twist stitches. Place a marker to indicate beginning of round.
Work the Cabled Rib Chart or Written Instructions for 8 rounds, being careful to twist the 7th and 8th stitches to the right rather than to the left.

Cabled Rib Chart

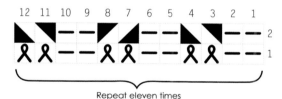

12 11 10 9 8 7 6 5 4 3 2 1

Repeat eleven times

Cabled Rib Written Instructions
Round 1: *P2, ktbl twice, p2, ktbl twice, p2, ktbl twice*, rep * to * 10 more times.
Round 2: *P2, t2l, p2, t2r, p2, t2l*, rep * to * 10 more times.

Switch to larger needles and begin working the Oak Knot Twist pattern.

Oak Knot Twist Chart (on page 30)

Oak Knot Twist Written Instructions
Round 1: *P2, ktbl twice, p2, ktbl, p4, ktbl*, rep * to * 10 more times.
Round 2: *P2, t2l, p2, ktbl, p4, ktbl*, rep * to * 10 more times.
Round 3: *P2, ktbl twice, p2, ktbl, p4, ktbl*, rep * to * 10 more times.
Round 4: *P1, t2r, t2l, p1, ktbl, p4, ktbl*, rep * to * 10 more times.
Round 5: *P1, ktbl, p2, ktbl, p1, ktbl, p4, ktbl*, rep * to * 10 more times.

Oak Knot Twist Chart

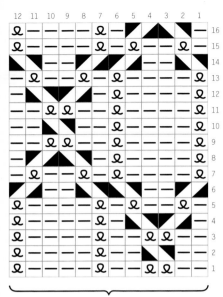

Repeat eleven times

Crown Decrease Chart

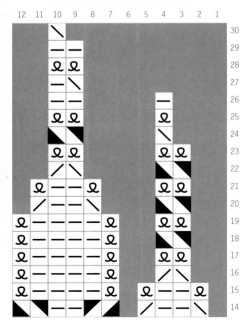

Round 6: *T2r, p2, t2l twice, p2, t2r*, rep * to * 10 more times.
Round 7: *Ktbl, p4, ktbl, p1, ktbl, p2, ktbl, p1*, rep * to * 10 more times.
Round 8: *Ktbl, p4, ktbl, p1, t2l, t2r, p1*, rep * to * 10 more times.
Round 9: *Ktbl, p4, ktbl, p2, ktbl twice, p2*, rep * to * 10 more times.
Round 10: *Ktbl, p4, ktbl, p2, t2l, p2*, rep * to * 10 more times.
Round 11: *Ktbl, p4, ktbl, p2, ktbl twice, p2*, rep * to * 10 more times.
Round 12: *Ktbl, p4, ktbl, p1, t2r, t2l, p1*, rep * to * 10 more times.
Round 13: *Ktbl, p4, ktbl, p1, ktbl, p2, ktbl, p1*, rep * to * 10 more times.
Round 14: *T2l, p2, t2r twice, p2, t2l*, rep * to * 10 more times.
Round 15: *P1, ktbl, p2, ktbl, p1, ktbl, p4, ktbl*, rep * to * 10 more times.
Round 16: *P1, t2l, t2r, p1, ktbl, p4, ktbl*, rep * to * 10 more times.

Repeat rounds 1-16 again.

Repeat rounds 1-13 once more and then follow the Crown Decrease Chart or Written Instructions.

Crown Decrease Chart (see below left)

Crown Decrease Written Instructions
Round 14: *Ssk, p2, k2tog, t2r, p2, t2l*, rep * to * 10 more times. 22sts dec, 110sts
Round 15: *Ktbl, p2, ktbl twice, p4, ktbl*, rep * to * 10 more times.
Round 16: *Ssk, k2tog, ktbl, p4, ktbl*, rep * to * 10 more times. 22sts dec, 88sts
Round 17: *Ktbl 3 times, p4, ktbl*, rep * to * 10 more times.
Round 18: *T2l, ktbl, p4, ktbl*, rep * to * 10 more times.
Round 19: *Ktbl 3 times, p4, ktbl*, rep * to * 10 more times.
Round 20: *T2l, ssk, p2, k2tog*, rep * to * 10 more times. 22sts dec, 66sts
Round 21: *Ktbl 3 times, p2, ktbl*, rep * to * 10 more times.
Round 22: *T2l, ssk, k2tog*, rep * to * 10 more times. 22sts dec, 44sts
Round 23: Knit all sts through the back loop.
Round 24: *Ssk, t2l*, rep * to * 10 more times. 11sts dec, 33sts
Round 25: Knit all sts through the back loop.
Round 26: Purl all sts.
Round 27: *Ssk, p1*, rep * to * 10 more times. 11sts dec, 22sts
Round 28: Knit all sts through the back loop.
Round 29: Purl all sts.
Round 30: Ssk 11 times. 11sts dec, 11sts

After the final round there will be 11sts. Cut the yarn, leaving a 25cm/10in tail and thread onto darning needle. Thread the yarn end through all the stitches twice and pull tight.
Weave in the yarn ends on inside of the hat. Block lightly.

knit with juno 'pearl' in velvet

sprinkle

A lot of people come into Loop wanting to knit a gender-neutral baby sweater. It can make people really nervous as they weigh up the associations of each colour. Yes, they could knit in white or cream, but for those knitters who love colour and want to explore fun combinations, we designed Sprinkle. It is especially fun to knit in one of Koigu's sprinkle colour combinations. You could choose a radical contrast to the sprinkle yarn or blend with one of its tones as we have done here.

Size: Finished chest size 50cm/20in, approx 3mos - 9mos

Yarn:
This pattern is suitable for most 4ply/fingering weight yarns. Look for one that is superwash, for easy baby care. It's a perfect pattern to use a handpainted plus a solid yarn, or mix one of Koigu's sprinkle yarns with a semi-solid.

Sprinkle version with stripes (opposite left):
Koigu Premium and Painter's Palette Premium Merino: 100% merino, 50g = 160m/175yd
Colour A: Koigu Premium Merino, semi-solid green - 2341, 1 skein
Colour B: Koigu Painter's Palette Premium Merino, sprinkle with green - P718, 1 skein

Alternate version without stripes (opposite right):
Quince & Co Tern: 75% wool, 25% silk, 50g = 202m/221yds
Colour A: Blue - Backbay, 1 skein
Colour B: Taupe - Driftwood, 1 skein

Gauge:
10cm/4in = 22sts x 48 rows in garter stitch
10cm/4in = 33sts x 30 rows in chevron stitch

(Chevron stitch grows in length and shrinks in width after it has been blocked. Measure gauge of chevron sample after washing and blocking it into shape.)

Needles:
3.75mm/US 5 circular or straight needles, as you prefer. If you decide to knit the sleeves in the round instead of flat, you will need 4 dpns or 100cm/40in circular for the 'magic loop' technique.

Notions: stitch holders or scrap yarn, darning needle, two 6mm/.25in buttons

Construction:
This sweater is worked from the bottom up to give the pointy shape to hems. The sleeves are knit to the underarm and then placed on stitch holders while the body is worked to the same point and then also placed on stitch holders. You can work the sleeves as flat pieces and seam them after joining to the body or work them in the round, whichever you prefer.
To join the sleeves to the yoke, the stitches for one of the cardigan fronts are picked up,

and then stitches for one sleeve, the stitches for the back of the cardigan, stitches for the second sleeve and the second front. Some stitches are reserved for the underarms from the cardigan body and sleeves. The yoke is knit and decreased into the garter stitch top.

Pattern:
Begin by making two sleeves. Follow *either* the flat sleeve instructions *or* sleeve in the round instructions. (These may also be used to test your gauge.)

To knit sleeve flat:
Cast on 58sts in Colour A and knit 5 rows in garter stitch.
Continue knitting, following the sleeve chart or written instructions for the ripple pattern, repeating the pattern between stitches 9-22, a total of 3 times. Work the four pattern rows a total of 6 times and then knit Rows 6 and 7 again. Cut yarn, leaving a 20cm/8in tail and place all the stitches on a holder or length of scrap yarn.

To knit sleeve in the round:
Sleeves in the round need no seam stitches, so should be worked as follows:
Cast on 56sts in Colour A, work 5 rounds of garter stitch, switch to Colour B. Work 1 round of 4 repeats of *k2tog, k4, kfb twice, k4, ssk*. Knit one round. Repeat these two rounds in Colour A.
Work these four rounds a total of 6 times and then repeat the first two rounds again.

Make second sleeve identically.

Flat Sleeve Written Instructions
Work all rows in Colour B if you are making the version without stripes.
Row 6 (RS): With Colour B, k1, kfb, k4, ssk, *k2tog, k4, kfb twice, k4, ssk*, rep * to * two more times, k2tog, k4, kfb, k1.
Row 7: Purl all stitches.
Row 8: With Colour A, k1, kfb, k4, ssk, *k2tog, k4, kfb twice, k4, ssk*, rep * to * two more times, k2tog, k4, kfb, k1.
Row 9: Purl all stitches.

Body
CO 162sts in Colour A. Knit 5 rows in garter stitch. You will always work four garter stitches on each cardigan edge; place a marker 4sts from each edge

sprinkle knit in koigu yarns with bambi shell buttons and version with no stripes made with quince & co. 'tern' using vintage buttons.

and always *knit* these edge stitches on both sides. The first 11sts will form the Left Front of the cardigan, and the last 11sts will be the Right Front of the cardigan.

For the striped version, work pattern Rows 6 & 7 in Colour B and Rows 8 & 9 in Colour A. For the alternate version without stripes, work all rows in Colour B. Stitches 12 - 25 on the chart show the pattern repeat, you may use markers to indicate these 14st intervals if you find this helpful. There are 10 repeats of these stitches, between the initial 11sts and last 11sts.

Knit 10 repeats of the four chart rows. Repeat Rows 6 & 7 once more.

Written Instructions for Chevron Body

For the alternate version with no stripes, work all rows in Colour B.

Row 6 (RS): With Colour B, k4, kfb, k4, ssk, *k2tog, k4, kfb twice, k4, ssk*, rep * to * 9 times more, k2tog, k4, kfb, k4.

Row 7: K4, p154, k4.

Row 8: With Colour A, k4, kfb, k4, ssk, *k2tog, k4, kfb twice, k4, ssk*, rep * to * 9 times more, k2tog, k4, kfb, k4.

Sleeve Ripple Pattern Chart

If knitting striped version, work Rows 6 & 7 in Colour B, and Rows 8 & 9 in Colour A.

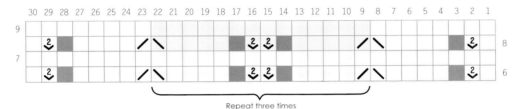

Repeat three times

Body Chevron Chart

Repeat ten times for body, repeat fourteen times when arms and body are joined

Row 9: K4, p154, k4.

Chevron Body Chart (see above)

Joining Arms and Body
You will now have knit two arms and the body up to the point where they join together into the yoke. At this point, we find it most helpful to run a spare piece of thin yarn through all the stitches on the body, as a 'lifeline', and to hold the stitches as they are remounted on the needles with the sleeves in the correct position.
Remount your stitches as follows, being careful to match the chevron stitch pattern across the shoulders:
With the RS facing pick up 39 Left Front stitches. In order for the pattern to match across the fronts, back and sleeves, pick up sleeve stitches from the same point in the chevron pattern where you left the body stitch pattern (at the end of a repeat, after ssk). If you have made your sleeves flat, line the edge up so it is under the arm. Pick up 42sts from the top of sleeve, beginning at the start of a pattern repeat, just before k2tog. You will be picking up 3 full pattern repeats on the sleeve. Fourteen stitches remain on hold for the sleeve underarm.
Skip 14sts for the underarm on the body and pick up 56sts from the back of the sweater. Repeat the same pick up pattern for the 42sts of the second sleeve, as you did for the first.
Leave 14 underarm stitches on holder and pick up 39sts for Right Front.
There are a total of 218sts on the needle.
Once the stitches are all back on the needles

continue Chevron pattern with Colour B, working Rows 8 & 9 of the Chart or Written Instructions, repeating chevron motif 14 times.
Repeat the four rows of Chevron Body pattern 3 more times.

Garter Yoke
Row 1: Change to Colour A, k4, *k2tog, k5*, rep * to * to last 4sts, k4. 188sts
Row 2: Knit all stitches.
Row 3: *K2tog, k1*, rep * to * to last 2sts, k2tog. 125sts
Row 4: Knit all stitches.
Row 5: K2, cast off 2sts to make buttonhole. Knit to the end of row.
Row 6: Knit across to bound off stitches. Turn knitting around and make 3sts with knitted cast on. Turn knitting around and slip the last new stitch on to left needle, k2tog, k1.
Rows 7-10: Knit all stitches.
Row 11: K4, *k2tog, k1*, rep * to * to last 5sts, k2tog, k3. 85sts
Rows 12-14: Knit all stitches.
Row 15-16: Rep Rows 5 & 6 to make second buttonhole.
Rows 17 and 18: Knit all stitches.
Row 19: K3, *k2tog, k1*, rep * to * to last 4sts, k2tog, k2. 58sts
Row 20: Knit all stitches.

Cast off knitwise. If you worked the sleeves flat stitch up the underarm seam so that the sleeve is now a tube. Graft underarm stitches together and weave in ends.
Wet block sweater to shape and dry flat.

brown eyed susan (three colour version) on
opposite page knit in the fibre company's
'acadia' in blue heron, bog and asparagus.
this page: loop, london. see page 98 for details.

brown-eyed susan

Brown-Eyed Susan is a crescent-shaped shawl with petal pleats at the bottom edge. It can be buttoned at the front, wrapped and tied at the back or draped around your neck. Brown-Eyed Susan can be made in as many or few colours as you choose. It can be knit in one solid colour, striped with a matching or contrast petal pleat border, or given a 'brown eye' by knitting the first twenty-three rows in a solid colour. Try working one of the stripes in a semi-solid and using leftover sock yarns for the alternating stripes.

Size: *S* (L); both sizes can be worked in a 4ply/fingering weight yarn or DK weight yarn

Yarn:
Small grey version (shown on page 53):
Viola Merino 4ply/Fingering: 100% superwash merino, 100g = 365m/400yd
Colour: Chimney Smoke, 1 skein
Finished measurements: width - 100cm/40in, depth - 33cm/13in

Small green and grey stripe version (shown on page 38):
The Fibre Company Acadia: 60% merino wool, 20% baby alpaca, 20% silk, 50g = 136m/149yd
Colour A: Blue Heron, 1 skein
Colour B: Bog, 1 skein
Colour C: Asparagus, 3 skeins
Finished measurements: width – 107cm/42in, depth – 42cm/16.5in

Large brown and pink stripe version (shown opposite):
madelinetosh Sock: 100% superwash merino, 100g = 361m/394yd

Colour A: William Morris, 2 skeins
Colour B: Trodden, 1 skein
Finished measurements: width - 185cm/73in, depth - 55cm/22in

Gauge:
4ply/fingering weight: 10cm/4in = 21sts x 34 rows st st
DK weight: 10cm/4in = 17sts x 26 rows in st st

Needles:
4ply/fingering weight version: 4mm/US 6
DK weight version: 4mm/US 6

Notions: stitch markers, darning needle, 3mm/D crochet hook

Notes:
Where directions apply to both sizes there is just one set of instructions, otherwise the small size is given in italics and the large size is given in parentheses.

The shawl is worked from the top-down and centre-out. You will be knitting a two-stitch garter border with M1 increases on the right and left sides

Try adding buttons for a different way of wearing your shawl. You don't need button holes, just use tiny buttons that will fit through the garter stitch edge.

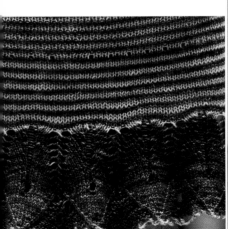

of a growing, crescent-shaped, striped stocking stitch centre.

M1 = In this pattern, 'make one' by working a yo and on the following row purl into the back of the yo twisting the stitch closed.

The phrase 'in pattern' refers to the following two-row pattern. Slip all markers as you come to them. There are two increases for each pair of rows:
RS: K2, yo, k to last 2sts, yo, k2.
WS: K2, ptbl, p to last 3sts, ptbl, k2.
If you are knitting the striped version, alternate colours every second row, so that you knit two rows in Colour A and two rows in Colour B. Do not over-tighten the stitches on the garter border, allowing the top edge to stretch as much as possible.
Where a new row total is the result of increases or decreases, the stitch count is given.

Pattern:
Using Colour A, CO 1st (a slip knot).
Row 1: Make 5sts in slip knot by working k1, yo, k1, yo, k1 through the slip knot.
Row 2: Knit all stitches.
Row 3 (WS): K2, yo twice, p1, yob twice, k2. 9sts
Switch to Colour B and alternate colours every second row if you wish to begin striping now or remain in Colour A until Row 25, if you want a 'brown eye'.
Row 4 (RS): K2, yo, k into the back of the first yob and k into the front of the second yob, k1, k into the back of the first yo and k in second yo, yo, k2. 11sts
Row 5: K2, yo, p to the last two sts, yob, k2. 13sts
Row 6: K2, yo, ktbl, (m1, k1) 8 times, yo, k2. 10sts inc; 23sts
Work in pattern, beginning with WS for 11 rows. 10sts inc; 33sts
Row 16 (RS): K2, yo, k1, m1, (k2, m1) six times, pm, k3, pm, (m1, k2) six times, m1, k1, yo, k2. The markers indicate the centre 3sts. 16sts inc; 49sts
Work in pattern, beginning with WS for 15 rows. 14sts inc; 63 sts
Row 32 (RS): K2, yo, *k2, m1*, rep * to * to marker, slm, k3, slm, *m1, k2*, rep * to * to last 2 sts, yo, k2. 30sts inc; 93sts

Work in pattern, beginning with WS row for 27 rows. 26sts inc; 119sts

Row 60 (RS): K2, yo, *k2, m1*, rep * to * to marker, slm,

k3, slm, *m1, k2*, rep * to * to last 2 sts, yo, k2. 58sts inc; 177 sts

Work in pattern, beginning with WS for 17 (47) rows.
16sts (46sts) inc; 193sts (223sts)

Small size: Row 78 (RS): Follow the Petal Pleat chart or written instructions in Colour A now.

Large size: Row 108 (RS): K2, yo, *k3, m1*, rep * to * to maker, slm, k3, slm, *m1, k3*, rep * to * to last 2sts, yo, k2. 74sts inc; 297sts

Work in pattern, beginning with WS for 29 rows. 28sts inc; 325sts. Begin Petal Pleat Chart or Written Instructions in Colour A.

Petal Pleat Chart (see following page)

Petal Pleat Written Instructions
Row 1 (RS): K2, *t2l, yo, k2, ssk, ptbl, k2tog, k2, yo*, rep * to * until last 4sts, t2l, k2. *193sts (325sts)*
Row 2 (WS): K2, ptbl twice, *p4, ktbl, p4, ptbl twice*, rep * to * until the last 2sts, k2.
Row 3: K2, *t2l, yo, k4, ptbl, k4, yo*, rep * to * until the last 4sts, t2l, k2. *34sts (58sts) inc; 227sts (383sts)*
Row 4: K2, ptbl twice, *p5, ktbl, p5, ptbl twice*, rep * to * until the last 2sts, k2.
Row 5: K2, *t2l, yo, k3, ssk, ptbl, k2tog, k3, yo*, rep * to * until the last 4sts, t2l k2.
Row 6: K2, ptbl twice, *p5, ktbl, p5, ptbl twice*, rep * to * until the last 2sts, k2.
Row 7: K2, *t2l, yo, k5, ptbl, k5, yo*, rep * to * until the last 4sts, t2l, k2. *34sts (58sts) inc; 261sts (441sts)*
Row 8: K2, ptbl twice, *p6, ktbl, p6, ptbl twice*, rep * to * until the last 2sts, k2.
Row 9: K2, *t2l, yo, k4, ssk, ptbl, k2tog, k4, yo*, rep * to * until the last 4sts, t2l, k2.
Row 10: K2, ptbl twice, *p6, ktbl, p6, ptbl twice*, rep * to * until the last 2sts, k2.
Row 11: K2, *t2l, yo, k6, ptbl, k6, yo *, rep * to * until the last 4sts, t2l, k2. *34sts (58sts) inc; 295sts (499sts)*
Row 12: K2, ptbl twice, *p7, ktbl, p7, ptbl twice*, rep * to * until the last 2sts, k2.
Row 13: K2, *t2l, yo, k5, ssk, ptbl, k2tog, k5, yo *, rep * to * until the last 4sts, t2l, k2.
Row 14: K2, ptbl twice, *p7, ktbl, p7, ptbl twice*, rep * to * until the last 2sts, k2.
Row 15: K2, *t2l, yo, k7, ptbl, k7, yo*, rep * to * until the last 4sts, t2l, k2. *34sts (58sts) inc; 329sts (557sts)*
Row 16: K2, ptbl twice, *p8, ktbl, p8, ptbl twice*, rep *

to * until the last 2sts, k2.
Row 17: K2, *t2l, yo, k6, ssk, ptbl, k2tog, k6, yo*, rep *
to * until the last 4sts, t2l, k2.
Row 18: K2, ptbl twice, *p8, ktbl, p8, ptbl twice*, rep *
to * until the last 2sts; k2.
Row 19: K2, *t2l, yo, k8, ptbl, k8, yo*, rep * to * until the
last 4sts, t2l, k2. *34sts (58sts) inc; 363sts (615sts)*
Row 20: K2, ptbl twice, *p9, ktbl, p9, ptbl twice*, rep *
to * until the last 2sts, k2.
Row 21: K2, yo, ssk, *yo, ssk, k7, k1w , k7, k2tog, yo,
ssk*, rep * to * until the last 2sts, yo, k2. *15sts (28sts)*

dec; *347sts (587sts)*
Row 22: K5, *p8, pkp in same st (m3), p8, k3*, rep * to
* until the last 2sts, k2. *34sts (58sts) inc; 381sts (645sts)*
Row 23: K2, *yo, k3, yo, ssk, k5, ssk, k1, k2tog, k5,
k2tog*, rep * to * until the last 5sts, yo, k3, yo, k2. *32sts
(56sts) dec; 349sts (589sts)*
Row 24: K7, *p15, k5*, rep * to * until the last 2sts, k2.
Row 25: K2, *yo, k5, yo, ssk, k11, k2tog*, rep * to * until
the last 7sts, yo, k5, yo, k2. *2sts inc; 351sts (591sts)*
Row 26: K9, *p13, k7*, rep * to * until the last 2sts, k2.
Row 27: K2, *yo, k2, k2tog, yo2, k3, yo, ssk, k9, k2tog*,

Petal Pleat Chart

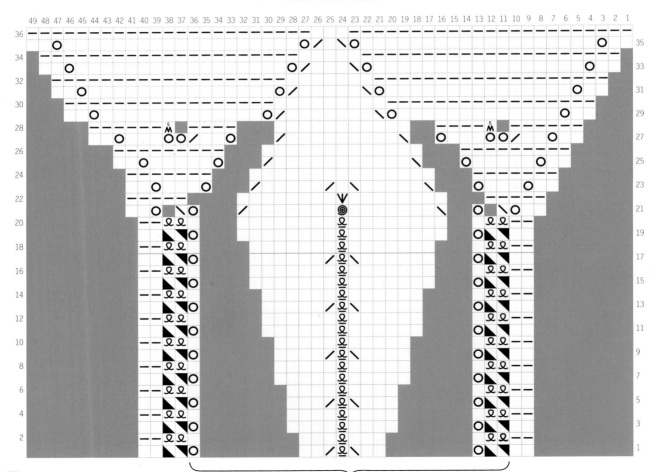

Repeat seventeen (twenty-nine) times

rep * to * until the last 9sts, yo, k2, k2tog, yo2, k3 yo, k2. *17sts (29sts) inc; 368sts (620sts)*

Row 28: K6, m5 in yo2, k4, *p11, k4, m5 in yo2, k4*, rep * to * until last 2sts, k2. *53sts (89sts) inc; 421sts (709sts)*

Row 29: K2, *yo, k13, yo, ssk, k7, k2tog*, rep * to * until the last 15 sts, yo, k13, yo, k2. *6sts inc; 427sts, (615sts)*

Row 30: K17, *p9, k15*, rep * to * until the last 2sts, k2.

Row 31: K2, *yo, k15, yo, ssk, k5, k2tog*, rep * to * until the last 17sts, yo, k15, yo, k2. *2sts inc; 429sts (717sts)*

Row 32: K19, *p7, k17*, rep * to * until the last 2sts, k2.

Row 33: K2, *yo, k17, yo, ssk, k3, k2tog*, rep * to * until the last 19sts, yo, k17, yo, k2. *2sts inc; 431sts (719sts)*

Row 34: K21, *p5, k19*, rep * to * until the last 2sts, k2.

Row 35: k2, *yo, k19, yo, ssk, k1, k2tog*, rep * to * until the last 21sts, yo, k19, yo, k2. *2sts inc; 433sts (721sts)*

Row 36: K23, *p3, k21*, rep * to * until the last 2sts, k2.

Crochet Cast Off

Cast off can be worked in contrasting or matching colour. If using a contrasting colour, cut the end of the last colour and begin crocheting with new colour, leaving a 15cm/6in tail for weaving in later. Place hook in last knit stitch, ch7, UKtr/USdc through 4 knit loops, [*ch7, UKtr/USdc through 3 knit loops*, rep * to * five more times, ch5, UKtr/USdc through 3 knit loops, ch5, UKtr/USdc through 3 knit loops], rep [ ] sequence across all petals. Ch7, UKtr/USdc through 4 knit loops.

Cut yarn and weave in ends.
Wet block gently to keep the shape of petal pleats.

crochet terms

The UK term 'treble crochet' and the US term 'double crochet' actually mean the same thing. For the edging, when you see the abbreviation UKtr/USdc, it means that you should insert the hook in the indicated knitted stitch loops, remove them from the knitting needle, yarn over hook, draw the yarn through the knitted stitch loops, yarn over and draw the yarn through both loops on hook to complete the stitch.

berry wrap

Size:
One size will fit most, however you can check the sizing as you near the end of knitting the body. If it looks like it will be too large or not large enough, change the length of the body by adding or subtracting from the total number of repeats. You will have to readjust the final knitted edging accordingly to accommodate. As a guide: neck edge = 60cm/24in, waist edge = 107cm/42in, body depth = 33cm/13in

Yarn:
Malabrigo Twist: 100% baby merino wool, 100g = 137m/149yd, 3 skeins
Colour shown: Damask Rose (see page 51)

Berroco Blackstone Tweed: 65% wool, 25% superkid mohair, 10% angora, 50g = 119m/130yd, 3 skeins
Colour shown: 2614 Cranberry Bog (shown right)

A wide variety of yarns can be used to make this wrap, which will cause the sizing to vary slightly. Worsted, aran, and aran chunky weight yarns are all suitable but needle size will need to be adjusted. Choose needle sizes so that the stocking stitch in the ties is firm and not too loose. You could also use a DK weight yarn held double.

Gauge:
Pink Malabrigo Twist version: 10cm/4in = 18st in stocking stitch with smaller needles
Red Blackstone Tweed version: 10cm/4in = 20st in stocking stitch with smaller needles

Needles:
Pink Malabrigo Twist version: 6mm/US 10 and 6.5mm/US 10.5 needles
Red Blackstone Tweed version: 5.5mm/US 9 and 6mm/US 10 needles

Notions: cable needle or spare dpn, darning needle, brooch (optional)

Note on Yarn Quantities:
To avoid breaking into a new ball of yarn just to finish off the last few rows of your wrap, mark your knitting with a pin when you are halfway through your yarn. This will be the centre back of the wrap. Knit the same amount of patterning again and then cast off. This way, you will be sure to have exactly enough yarn to finish the project without waste.

Construction:
The first tie end is knit and then the stitches are increased into the patterned Berry Stitch body of the wrap. Once all the body stitches are worked, they are cast off. The second tie end is knit and sewn to the cast off edge of the wrap. A small flap is knitted to the wrong side of the second tie end, to feed the first end through. You can use a brooch on top for added decoration. Finally, a knitted edge is worked along the wide garter neck edge to gather and add shape to the neckline.

Pattern
CO 4sts with smaller needles.

Follow Tie End with Pleat Decrease chart or written instructions.

Tie End with Pleat Decrease Written Instructions
Rows 1 (RS) & 2 (WS): K4.
Row 3: K1, m1, k2, m1, k1.
Row 4: K6.
Row 5: K2, m1, k2, m1, k2. 8sts
Row 6: K8.
Row 7: K3, m1, k2, m1, k3. 10st
Row 8: K3, p4, k3.
Row 9: K4, m1, k2, m1, k4. 12sts

Tie End with Pleat Decrease Chart

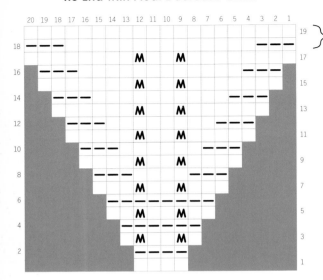

Row 10: K3, p6, k3.
Row 11: K5, m1, k2, m1, k5. 14sts
Row 12: K3, p8, k3.
Row 13: K6, m1, k2, m1, k6. 16sts
Row 14: K3, p10, k3.
Row 15: K7, m1, k2, m1, k7. 18sts
Row 16: K3, p12, k3.
Row 17: K8, m1, k2, m1, k8. 20sts
Row 18: K3, p14, k3.
Row 19: K20.

Repeat Rows:
Repeat Rows 18 and 19 nine more times.
Work Row 18 once more.

Work Decrease Pleat:
Next Row (RS): Create decrease pleat by putting the first 5sts on a cable needle or spare dpn and with RS still facing, hold to the front of the knitting. Knit the first stitch from the cable needle together with the first stitch on knitting needle (decreasing 1st). Repeat this for each of the stitches on the cable needle. You will have decreased 5sts.
Put the next 5sts on the cable needle and hold at the back of the knitting. Knit the first stitch on needle together with the first stitch on cable needle (decreasing 1st). Do this for each of the stitches.

You will have 10sts when you have completed this row.

Next Row (WS): K3, p4, k3.
Next Row (RS): K10.

Repeat these 2 rows five more times. Repeat the WS row one more time.

Now follow the chart or written instructions for tie widening as below.

Tie Widening:
Row 1 (RS): K4, m1, k2, m1, k4. 12sts
Row 2: K3, p6, k3.
Row 3: K5, m1, k2, m1, k5. 14sts
Row 4: K3, p8, k3.
Row 5: K6, m1, k2, m1, k6. 16sts
Row 6: K3, p10, k3.
Row 7: K7, m1, k2, m1, k7. 18sts
Row 8: K3, p12, k3.
Row 9: K8, m1, k2, m1, k8. 20sts
Row 10: K3, p14, k3.
Row 11: K9, m1, k2, m1, k9. 22sts
Row 12: K3, p16, k3.
Row 13: K10, m1, k2, m1, k10. 24sts
Row 14: K3, p18, k3.

Tie Widening Chart

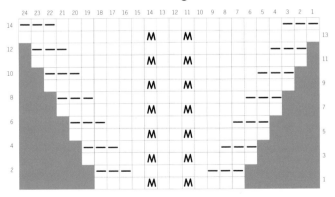

Wrap Body:
Switch to larger needles.

The body of the wrap has a border of 5sts of garter on the neckline edge and a single garter stitch at the bottom edge. There are three columns of textured pattern, divided by columns of 3-stitch-wide garter.

Berry Stitch Chart

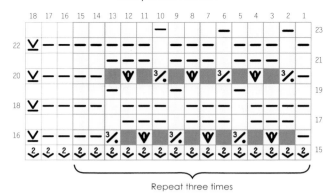

18 17 16 15 14 13 12 11 10 9 8 7 6 5 4 3 2 1

Repeat three times

Finishing
Make second tie end following the instructions for the first one finishing with Row 14 of tie widening. Cast off knitwise. Sew to cast off edge of wrap.

Fold each tie end in half and sew cast-on edge to the wrong side, creating a bell shape. This makes the tie weightier so that it hangs well.

Make a tie flap on the second tie as follows:
Pick up 10sts on the back of the flap (see illustration below), where there are 10st sts between the garter edges. Knit 14 rows in stocking stitch. Cast off knitwise and sew the flap down flat to the back of the tie so that it covers its narrowest part.

Knitted Edging
The knitted edging is only on the edge with the wider band of garter stitch. It will gather the wrap closely around your shoulders.

With RS of work facing, beginning on the garter edge of the Berry Stitch, after the ties, pick up and knit 2sts. Cast off 1st st by pulling over 2nd stitch. Work 3 more stitches this way. Then decrease by skipping one edge stitch each time you pick up and knit a stitch. Continue to skip an edge stitch and pick up in the next one until there are only 4 edge stitches left. Pick up, knit and cast off in each of these. Cut yarn and weave in all ends. Wet block and wear.

The first row increases to 48sts. Place markers where instructed when you begin Berry Stitch at Row 16. After this row, slip the markers every row. The pattern becomes easy to remember after about 2 repeats.

Follow chart or written instructions for Berry Stitch, placing markers between repeats.

Berry Stitch Written Instructions
Row 15 (RS): Kfb in each st. 48sts
Row 16 (WS): S1wyif, k2, [k2, *p3tog, (k1, yo, k1) in same st,* rep * to * two more times, k1, pm], rep [ ] two more times, omitting last slm.
Row 17: [K1, *p3, k1*, rep * to * two more times, k2, slm], rep [ ] two more times, slm, k3.
Row 18: S1wyif, k2, [k2, *p1, k3*, rep * to * once more, p1, k4, slm], rep [ ] two more times, omitting last slm.
Row 19: [K4, *p1, k3*, rep * to * once more, p1, k2, slm], rep [ ] two more times, slm, k3.
Row 20: S1wiyif, k2, [k2, *(k1, yo, k1) in same st, p3tog*, rep * to * two more times, k1, slm], rep [ ] two more times, omitting last slm.
Row 21: [K2, *p3, k1*, rep * to * two more times, k1, slm], rep [ ] two more times, slm, k3.
Row 22: S1wyif, k2, [k5, *p1, k3*, rep * to * once more, p1,k1, slm], rep [ ] two more times, omitting last slm.
Row 23: [K1,*p1, k3*, rep * to * two more times, k2, slm], rep [ ] two more times, k3.

Repeat rows 16-23 until the textured body measures 107cm/42in long (or desired length), ending with Row 19.
Next Row: K2tog across. 24sts
Cast off purlwise.

making the tie flap

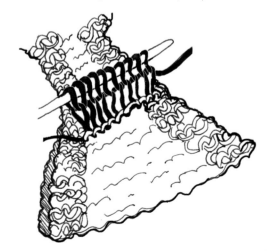

swatches of hand ~ dyed yarn from viola
opposite left: brown ~ eyed susan (one colour version, page forty)
knit with viola 'fingering' in chimney smoke. opposite right:
prairie shawl (page eighteen) knit with dyeforyarn 'merino and
mulberry silk' in antique doll

swoon

This delicate sweater was designed as a layering piece for any weather. It's like wearing an airy lace shawl without having to worry about how it stays on.

Size: One size fits most (see diagram below)

Yarn:
madelinetosh Prairie: 100% superwash merino wool, 100g = 768m/840yd, 2 skeins
Colour shown: Composition Book Grey

Gauge:
10cm/4in = 22sts x 40 rows in Wrapped Stocking Stitch

Needles:
3.75mm/US 5, 100cm/40in circular needle

Notions: smooth scrap yarn in contrasting colour, darning needle

Note on Construction:
This sweater is knit from the top down. Temporary stitches are cast on for the back, which is knit down to the underarm. The fronts are picked up from the back shoulder stitches and knit down to the same point, where the three pieces are joined together to knit from the armholes to the hem, including the bobble ruffle edging. The lace neckline and sleeves are knit separately and sewn on.

Pattern:

Back
Using scrap yarn, CO 179sts with provisional cast on. Follow the 24 rows of chart or written instructions for Wrapped Stocking Stitch.

Repeat the 24 rows of Wrapped Stocking Stitch once more and then knit the first twelve rows of sequence again (60 rows). You have arrived at the underarm. Put all back stitches on a holder and work fronts to the underarm.

Wrapped Stocking Stitch Chart (see following page)

Wrapped Stocking Stitch Written Instructions
Rows 1, 3 & 5 (RS): Knit all sts.
Rows 2, 4 & 6 (WS): Purl all sts.
Row 7 (RS): K4, *3sw, k11*, rep * to * eleven more times, 3sw, k4.
Rows 8-18: Work in st st.
Row 19 (RS): K11, *3sw, k11*, rep * to * eleven more times.
Rows 20-24: Work in st st

Right Front
Working on the right shoulder of the back (as it would be worn) pick up 74sts with the RS of fabric facing, so that your needle point comes out at right shoulder. Follow the chart or written

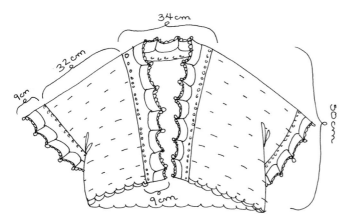

34cm

32cm

9cm

50cm

9cm

Wrapped Stocking Stitch Chart

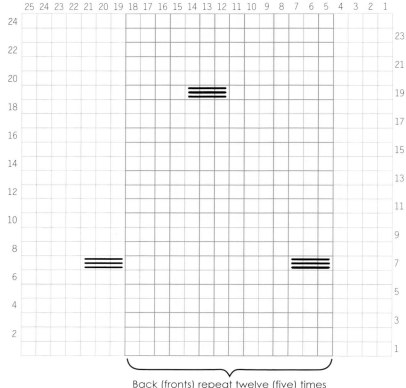

Back (fronts) repeat twelve (five) times
When body is joined after armhole, repeat twenty-three times

would be worn) pick up 74sts with the RS of fabric facing, so that your needle point comes out at neckline. Work Rows 13-24 of chart or written instructions for Wrapped Stocking Stitch.

Repeat the 24 rows of the Left Front Wrapped Stocking Stitch twice more (60 rows). You have arrived at the underarm.

Left Front Written Instructions
Begin this section at Row 13.
Rows 1, 3 & 5 (RS): Knit all sts.
Rows 2, 4 & 6 (WS): Purl all sts.
Row 7 (RS): K4, *3sw, k11*, rep * to * four more times, 3sw, k4.
Rows 8, 10, 12, 14, 16 & 18 (WS): Purl all sts.
Rows 9, 11, 13, 15,17 (RS): Knit all sts.
Row 19 (RS): K11, *3sw, k11*, rep * to * four more times.
Rows 20-24: Work in st st.

Joining at the Underarm
Beginning at the Left Front neckline, knit pattern Row 1 for 74sts. Cast on 3sts using backward loop method. Continuing in pattern, knit 179 back sts. Cast on 3sts. Knit the final 74sts of Right Front in pattern (333sts).

Body Instructions
Resume pattern Rows 2-24, following Wrapped Stocking Stitch chart or written instructions.
Repeat the 24 rows of the Wrapped Stocking Stitch written instructions or chart once more and then repeat rows 1-12 again. Continue on to Double Bobble Edge using the chart (refer to Row 1 of written instructions for guidence)or written instructions.

Double Bobble Edge Written Instructions
Row 1 (RS): Use a length of scrap yarn in a contrasting colour to weave in and out of the stitches as you knit them, so that you can find the pick up row easily. With scrap yarn held at back, knit first stitch with working yarn. Bring scrap yarn to front, knit second stitch with working yarn. Repeat to the end of row.

instructions for Wrapped Stocking Stitch, Rows 1-24. Repeat the 24 rows of Wrapped Stocking Stitch once more and then knit Rows 1-12 again (60 rows). You have arrived at the underarm. Break yarn and put all right front stitches on hold.

Right Front Written Instructions
Rows 1, 3 & 5 (RS): Knit all sts.
Rows 2, 4 & 6 (WS): Purl all sts.
Row 7 (RS): K4, *3sw, k11*, rep * to * four more times, 3sw, k4.
Rows 8-18: Work in st st.
Row 19 (RS): K11, *3sw, k11*, rep * to * four more times.
Rows 20-24: Work in st st.

Left Front
Working on the left shoulder of the back (as it

Double Bobble Edge Chart

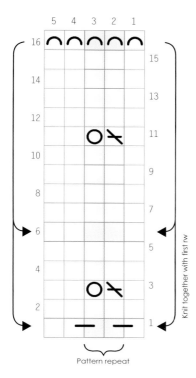

Pattern repeat

Knit together with first rw

Row 2 (WS): Purl all sts.
Row 3 (RS): K1, *k2tog tbl, yo*, rep * to * to last 2 sts, k2.
Row 4: Purl all sts.
Row 5: Knit all sts.
Row 6: You will now pick up the tops of the stitches from Row 1 and purl them together with the stitches in this row, one at a time. Use the woven thread to help you locate the right stitches to pick up. You are actually picking up the top of the stitch from below Row 1. Look for the first purl bump below the woven thread and place this onto your left needle purlwise and p2tog with your 1st stitch from Row 6. Continue along the row, picking up a stitch from below Row 1 and purling it together with a stitch from this row, so that each of the stitches in the first row is knit together with a stitch from this row, creating a welt. (see blog for tips)
Rows 7-10: Work in st st.
Row 11 (RS): K1, *k2tog tbl, yo*, rep * to * to last 2 sts,k2.
Rows 12-15: Work in st st.

Row 16: You will now be knitting the stitches from this row together with the same stitches that you picked up before and then casting them off. Look for the stitches that have two strands, these are the ones you picked up previously. Pick up the first stitch from below Row 1 and purl it together with first st from final row. Repeat. Slip both right needle stitches to the left needle and p2tog. Continue along row so that each of the stitches in the first row is purled together with a stitch from this row and then bound off, creating a second welt or hem. Pull on the peaked yo edges to get the hem and peaks to form properly.

Lace Collar & Sleeves
The collar and sleeve lace trims start with a picot hem and then knit towards the straight edge that will be sewn to the garment.

Lace Collar
CO 283sts and knit following the chart or written instructions for Lace Edging.

Lace Sleeves
CO 143sts and knit following the chart or written instructions for Lace Edging. Make two the same.

Lace Edging Chart (see following page)

Lace Edging Written Instructions
Repeats are given for the collar and (sleeves).

Rows 1&3 (RS): Knit all sts.
Rows 2&4 (WS): K1, p to last st, k1.
Row 5: K1, *k2tog tbl, yo*, rep * to * until the last 2sts, k2.
Rows 6&8: K1, p to last st, k1.
Rows 7&9: Knit all sts.
Row 10: You will now pick up the cast on edge stitches and purl them together with the stitches in this row, one at a time. Place the first CO stitch on your left needle purl-wise and k2tog with the first st from Row 10 (the first and last stitches are the only ones to be k2tog, the rest are p2tog). Continue along the row, picking up a CO stitch and purling it together with a stitch from this row, so that each of the stitches in the first row is worked together with a CO edge stitch, creating a picot hem.
Row 11: K1, ssk, *k5, yo, k1, yo, k5, cdd*, rep * to * 18 (8) more times, k5, yo, k1, yo, k5, k2tog, k1.
Row 12: K1, p6, k3, *p11, k3*, rep * to * 18 (8) more times, p6, k1.

Lace Edging Chart

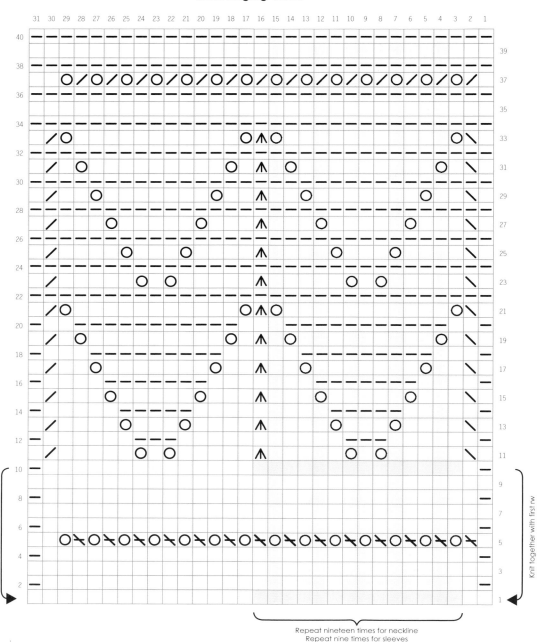

Repeat nineteen times for neckline
Repeat nine times for sleeves

Knit together with first rw

Row 13: K1, ssk, *k4, yo, k3, yo, k4, cdd*, rep * to * 18 (8) more times, k4, yo, k3, yo, k4, k2tog, k1.
Row 14: K1, p5, k5, *p9, k5*, rep * to * 18 (8) more times, p5, k1.
Row 15: K1, ssk, *k3, yo, k5, yo, k3, cdd*, rep * to * 18 (8) more times, k3, yo, k5, yo, k3, k2tog, k1.
Row 16: K1, p4, k7, *p7, k7*, rep * to * 18 (8) more times, p4, k1.
Row 17: K1, ssk, *k2, yo, k7, yo, k2, cdd*, rep * to * 18 (8) more times, k2, yo, k7, yo, k2, k2tog, k1.
Row 18: K1, p3, k9, *p5, k9*, rep * to * 18 (8) more times, p3, k1.
Row 19: K1, ssk, *k1, yo, k9, yo, k1, cdd*, rep * to * 18 (8) more times, k1, yo, k9, yo, k1, k2tog, k1.
Row 20: K1, p2, k11, *p3, k11*, rep * to * 18 (8) more times, p2, k1.
Row 21: K1, ssk, *yo, k11, yo, cdd*, rep * to * 18 (8) more times, yo, k11, yo, k2tog, k1.

Row 22 and all following even numbered rows (WS): Knit all sts.

Row 23: K1, ssk, *k5, yo, k1, yo, k5, cdd*, rep * to * 18 (8) more times, k5, yo, k1, yo, k5, k2tog, k1.
Row 25: K1, ssk, *k4, yo, k3, yo, k4, cdd*, rep * to * 18 (8) more times, k4, yo, k3, yo, k4, k2tog, k1.
Row 27: K1, ssk, *k3, yo, k5, yo, k3, cdd*, rep * to * 18 (8) more times, k3, yo, k5, yo, k3, k2tog, k1.
Row 29: K1, ssk, *k2, yo, k7, yo, k2, cdd*, rep * to * 18 (8) more times, k2, yo, k7, yo, k2, k2tog, k1.
Row 31: K1, ssk, *k1, yo, k9, yo, k1, cdd*, rep * to * 18 (8) more times, k1, yo, k9, yo, k1, k2tog, k1.
Row 33: K1, ssk, *yo, k11, yo, cdd*, rep * to * 18 (8) more times, yo, k11, yo, k2tog, k1.
Row 35: Knit all sts.
Row 37: K1, *k2tog, yo*, rep * to * to last 2sts, k2.
Row 39: Knit all sts
Row 40: Knit all sts.

Cast off knitwise.

Attaching the Lace Collar
Attach the collar by sewing the cast off edge to the sweater neckline. Fold the collar in half to find the centre point and mark with a stitch marker or spare yarn. Pin (or tie with spare yarn) the centre back of collar to the centre back of sweater neckline. Pin the bottom edges of the collar to the bottom edge of sweater. Pin the rest of the collar in place, easing excess collar fabric around the back neckline. When the stitches look evenly distributed,

sew the collar on using mattress stitch.

Attaching the Lace Sleeves
Sew the underarm seams of the sleeves closed using mattress stitch. Position the underarm seam at the underarm of sweater armhole and pin in place. Find the midway point of the sleeve caps and the sweater shoulders and pin them together. Distribute the rest of the stitches evenly across the armhole, positioning any excess sleeve stitches towards the sleeve cap. Sew the lace sleeves in place using mattress stitch.

To finish the sweater, weave in loose ends and wet block.

elk in the woods

The inspiration for these came from our own winter wardrobes. A lot of our clothes are loose fitting, with low necklines and short sleeves, which can sometimes be a little drafty. The neck wrap and wrist warmers are small pieces, perfect for using up odd amounts of left over yarn. They could be dk yarns as well, since the size isn't too crucial. Close the neck wrap with a shawl pin or pretty brooch.

Yarn:
madelinetosh Pashmina: 75% superwash wool, 15% silk, and 10% cashmere, 100g = 329m/360yds, 1 skein
Colour shown: Tern

Gauge:
These are small projects and gauge isn't crucial, so you can dive right in with an estimated needle size. After you have knit one repeat of the pattern, you can check your gauge and either carry on or start again with another needle size if you feel it is necessary. The gauge is measured over the centre of the panel, on the reverse stocking stitch with twist stitches.

Neck Wrap: centre panel measures 5cm/2in at narrowest part and 6cm/2.25in at widest
Wrist Warmers: centre panel measures 4.5cm/1.75in at narrowest part and 5.5cm/2.25in at widest

Needles:
The Neck Wrap is worked on larger needles to create better drape, while the Wrist Warmers are knit on smaller needles to scale down the size and keep your wrists cosy.
4mm/US 6 straight or circular needles for Neck Wrap
2.75mm/US 2 straight or circular needles for Wrist Warmers

Notions: cable needle, darning needle, 2 approx. 11.5mm/.45in buttons for wrist warmers - we used Oblong Mirror Glass buttons. Neck Wrap -brooch.

Pattern:

Neck Wrap
Using larger needles, CO 21sts using cable method. Working from charts or written instructions, knit rows 1-50 of Neck Warmer and then repeat Rows 23-50 five more times.
Work the rows from the Neck Wrap End using chart (see page 62) or written instructions.
After the final stitch, fasten off and darn in yarn ends. Wet block, gently shaping your edge leaves with your hand, rather than pinning.

Neck Wrap Chart (see following page)

Neck Wrap Written instructions
Rows 1 and 3 (RS): K1, *ktbl, p1*, rep * to * 8 more times, ktbl, k1. 21sts
Row 2 and 4 (WS): P1, *s1wyif, k1*, rep * to * 8 more times, s1wyif, p1. 21sts
Row 5: K1, ktbl, p7, t3f, p7, ktbl, k1.
Row 6: P1, s1wyif, k7, s1wyif, k1, s1wyif, k7, s1wyif, p1.
Row 7: K1, ktbl, p6, t2b, p1, t2f, p6, ktbl, k1.
Row 8: P1, s1wyif, k6, s1wyif, k3, s1wyif, k6, s1wyif, p1.

Row 9: K1, ktbl, p5, t2b, p3, t2f, p5, ktbl, k1.
Row 10: P1, *s1wyif, k5*, rep * to * three times, s1wyif, p1.
Row 11: K1, ktbl, p4, t2b, p5, t2f, p4, ktbl, k1.
Row 12: P1, s1wyif, k4, s1wyif, k7, s1wyif, k4, s1wyif, p1.
Row 13: K1, ktbl, p3, t2r, p7, t2l, p3, ktbl, k1.
Row 14: P1, s1wyif, k3, s2wyif, k7, s2wyif, k3, s1wyif, p1.
Row 15: K1, ktbl, p2, t2b, t2f, p5, t2b, t2f, p2, ktbl, k1.
Row 16: P1, (s1wyif, k2) twice, s1wyif, k5, (s1wyif, k2)

twice, s1wyif, p1.
Row 17: K1, ktbl, p1, t2b, p2, t2f, p3, t2b, p2, t2f, p1, ktbl, k1.
Row 18: P1, s1wyif, k1, s1wyif, k4, s1wyif, k3, s1wyif, k4, s1wyif, k1, s1wyif, p1.
Row 19: K1, ktbl, t2b, p4, t2f, p1, t2b, p4, t2f, ktbl, k1.
Row 20: P1, s2wyif, k6, s1wyif, k1, s1wyif, k6, s2wyif, p1.
Row 21: K1, t2r, p6, t3f, p6, t2l, k1.

Row 22: K1, s2wyif, yo, k6, s1wyif, k1, s1wyif, k6, yo, s2wyif, k1. 24sts
Row 23: K1, yo, ktbl, yo2, ktbl, p6, t2b, p1, t2f, p6, ktbl, yo2, ktbl, yo, k1. 27sts
Row 24: K2, s1wyif, p1, k1, s1wyif, k6, s1wyif, k3, s1wyif, k6, s1wyif, k1, p1, s1wyif, k2.
Row 25: K2, yo, ktbl, yo, k2, ktbl, p5, t2b, p3, t2f, p5, ktbl, k2, yo, ktbl, yo, k2. 31sts
Row 26: K3, s1wyif, k3, s1wyif, k5, s1wyif, k5, s1wyif, k5, s1wyif, k3, s1wyif, k3.
Row 27: K3, yo, ktbl, yo, k3, ktbl, p4, t2r, p5, t2l, p4, ktbl, k3, yo, ktbl, yo, k3. 35sts
Row 28: K4, s1wyif, k4, s1wyif, k4, s2wyif, k5, s2wyif, k4, s1wyif, k4, s1wyif, k4.
Row 29: K4, yo, ktbl, yo, k4, ktbl, p3, t2b, t2f, p3, t2b, t2f, p3, ktbl, k4, yo, ktbl, yo, k4. 39sts
Row 30: K5,

Neck Wrap Chart

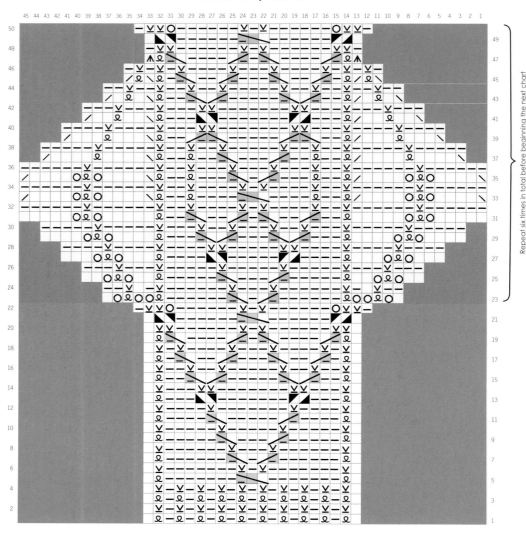

Repeat six times in total before beginning the next chart

Neck End Chart

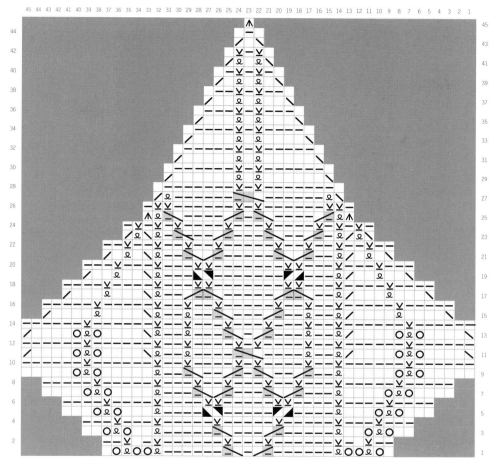

s1wyif, k5, (s1wyif, k3, s1wyif, k2) twice, s1wyif, k3, (s1wyif, k5) twice.

Row 31: K5, yo, ktbl, yo, k5, ktbl, p2, t2b, p2, t2f, p1, t2b, p2, t2f, p2, ktbl, k5, yo, ktbl, yo, k5. 43sts

Row 32: K6, s1wyif, k6, s1wyif, k2, s1wyif, k4, s1wyif, k1, s1wyif, k4, s1wyif, k2, s1wyif, k6, s1wyif, k6.

Row 33: Ssk, k4, yo, ktbl, yo, k4, k2tog, ktbl, p2, ktbl, p4, t3f, p4, ktbl, p2, ktbl, ssk, k4, yo, ktbl, yo, k4, k2tog.

Row 34: K6, s1wyif, k6, s1wyif, k2, s1wyif, k4, s1wyif, k1, s1wyif, k4, s1wyif, k2, s1wyif, k6, s1wyif, k6.

Row 35: Ssk, k4, yo, ktbl, yo, k4, k2tog, ktbl, p2, ktbl,

p3, t2b, p1, t2f, p3, ktbl,p2, ktbl, ssk, k4, yo, ktbl,yo, k4, k2tog.

Row 36: K6, s1wyif, k6, s1wyif, k2, (s1wyif, k3) three times, s1wyif, k2, s1wyif, k6, s1wyif, k6.

Row 37: Ssk, k4, ktbl, k4, k2tog, ktbl, p2, ktbl, p2, t2b, p3, t2f, p2, ktbl, p2, ktbl, ssk, k4, ktbl, k4, k2tog. 39sts

Row 38: K5, s1wyif, k5, s1wyif, k2, s1wyif, k2, s1wyif, k5, s1wyif, k2, s1wyif, k2, s1wyif, k5, s1wyif, k5.

Row 39: Ssk, k3, ktbl, k3, k2tog, ktbl, p2, t2f, t2b, p5, t2f, t2b, p2, ktbl, ssk, k3, ktbl, k3, k2tog. 35sts

Row 40: K4, s1wyif, k4, s1wyif, k3, s2wyif, k7, s2wyif, k3, s1wyif, k4, s1wyif, k4.

Row 41: Ssk, k2, ktbl, k2, k2tog, ktbl, p3, t2r, p7, t2l, p3, ktbl, ssk, k2, ktbl, k2, k2tog. 31sts

Row 42: K3, s1wyif, k3, s1wyif, k3, s2wyif, k7, s2wyif, k3, s1wyif, k3, s1wyif, k3.

Row 43: Ssk, k1, ktbl, k1, k2tog, ktbl, p2, t2b, t2f, p5, t2b, t2f, p2, ktbl, ssk, k1, ktbl, k1, k2tog. 27sts

Row 44: K2, (s1wyif, k2) three times, s1wyif, k5, (s1wyif, k2) four times.

Row 45: Ssk, ktbl, k2tog, ktbl, p1, t2b, p2, t2f, p3, t2b, p2, t2f, p1, ktbl, ssk, ktbl, k2tog. 23sts

Row 46: K1, s1wyif, k1, s1wyif, k1, s1wyif, k4, s1wyif, k3, s1wyif, k4, s1wyif, k1, s1wyif, k1, s1wyif, k1.

Row 47: Cdd, ktbl, t2b, p4, t2f, p1, t2b, p4, t2f, ktbl, cdd. 21sts

Row 48: K1, s2wyif, k6, s1wyif, k1, s1wyif, k6, s2wyif, k1.

Row 49: K1, t2r, p6, t3f, p6, t2l, k1.

Row 50: K1, s2wyif, yo, k6, s1wyif, k1, s1wyif, k6, yo, s2wyif, k1. 23sts

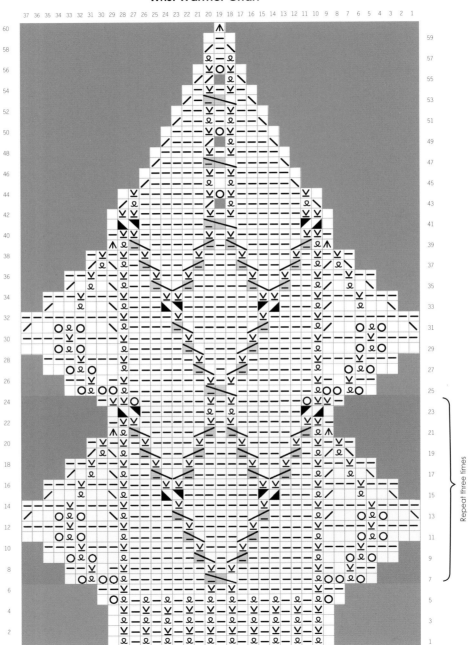

Neck Wrap End chart (see page 63)

Neck Wrap End Written instructions

Row 1 (RS): K1, yo, ktbl, yo2, ktbl, p6, t2b, p1, t2f, p6, ktbl, yo2, ktbl, yo, k1. 29sts

Row 2 (WS): K2, s1wyif, p1, k1, s1wyif, k6, s1wyif, k3, s1wyif, k6, s1wyif, k1, p1, s1wyif, k2.

Row 3: K2, yo, ktbl, yo, k2, ktbl, p5, t2b, p3, t2f, p5, ktbl, k2, yo, ktbl, yo, k2. 33sts

Row 4: K3, s1wyif, k3, s1wyif, k5, s1wyif, k5, s1wyif, k5, s1wyif, k3, s1wyif, k3.

Row 5: K3, yo, ktbl, yo, k3, ktbl, p4, t2r, p5, t2l, p4, ktbl, k3, yo, ktbl, yo, k3. 37sts

Row 6: K4, s1wyif, k4, s1wyif, k4, sl2 wyif, k5, sl2 wyif, k4, s1wyif, k4, s1wyif, k4.

Row 7: K4, yo, ktbl, yo, k4, ktbl, p3, t2b, t2f, p3, t2b, t2f, p3, ktbl, k4, yo, ktbl, yo, k4. 41sts

Row 8: K5, s1wyif, k5, s1wyif, k3, s1wyif, k2, s1wyif, k3, s1wyif, k2, s1wyif, k3, s1wyif, k5, s1wyif, k5.

Row 9: K5, yo, ktbl, yo, k5, ktbl, p2, t2b, p2, t2f, p1, t2b, p2, t2f, p2, ktbl, k5, yo, ktbl, yo, k5. 45sts.

Row 10: K6, s1wyif, k6, s1wyif, k2, s1wyif, k4, s1wyif, k1, s1wyif, k4, s1wyif, k2, s1wyif, k6, s1wyif, k6.

Row 11: Ssk, k4, yo, ktbl, yo, k4, k2tog, ktbl, p2, ktbl, p4, t3f, p4, ktbl, p2, ktbl, ssk, k4, yo, ktbl, yo, k4, k2tog.

Row 12: K6, s1wyif, k6, s1wyif, k2, s1wyif, k4, s1wyif, k1, s1wyif, k4, s1wyif, k2, s1wyif, k6, s1wyif, k6.

Row 13: Ssk, k4, yo, ktbl, yo, k4, k2tog, ktbl, p2, ktbl, p3, t2b, p1, t2f, p3, ktbl, p2, ktbl, ssk, k4, yo, ktbl, yo, k4, k2tog.

Row 14: K6, s1wyif, k6, s1wyif, k2, s1wyif, k3, s1wyif, k3, s1wyif, k3, s1wyif, k2, s1wyif, k6, s1wyif, k6.

Row 15: Ssk, k4, ktbl, k4, k2tog, ktbl, p2, ktbl, p2, t2b, p3, t2f, p2, ktbl, p2, ktbl, ssk, k4, ktbl, k4, k2tog. 41sts

Row 16: K5, s1wyif, k5, s1wyif, k2, s1wyif, k2, s1wyif, k5, s1wyif, k2, s1wyif, k2, s1wyif, k5, s1wyif, k5.

Row 17: Ssk, k3, ktbl, k3, k2tog, ktbl, p2, t2f, t2b, p5, t2f, t2b, p2, ktbl, ssk, k3, ktbl, k3, k2tog. 37sts

Row 18: K4, s1wyif, k4, s1wyif, k3, s2wyif, k7, s2wyif, k3, s1wyif, k4, s1wyif, k4.

Row 19: Ssk, k2, ktbl, k2, k2tog, ktbl, p3, t2r, p7, t2l, p3, ktbl, ssk, k2, ktbl, k2, k2tog. 33sts

Row 20: K3, s1wyif, k3, s1wyif, k3, s2wyif, k7, s2wyif, k3, s1wyif, k3, s1wyif, k3.

Row 21: Ssk, k1, ktbl, k1, k2tog, ktbl, p2, t2b, t2f, p5, t2b, t2f, p2, ktbl, ssk, k1, ktbl, k1, k2tog. 29sts

Row 22: K2, s1wyif, k2, s1wyif, k2, s1wyif, k2, s1wyif, k5, s1wyif, k2, s1wyif, k2, s1wyif, k2, s1wyif, k2.

Row 23: Ssk, ktbl, k2tog, ktbl, p1, t2b, p2, t2f, p3, t2b, p2, t2f, p1, ktbl, ssk, ktbl, k2tog. 25sts

Row 24: K1, s1wyif, k1, s1wyif, k1, s1wyif, k4, s1wyif, k3, s1wyif, k4, s1wyif, k1, s1wyif, k1, s1wyif, k1.

Row 25: Cdd, ktbl, t2b, p5, t2f, p1, t2b, p4, t2f, ktbl, cdd. 21sts

Row 26: K1, s2wyif, k6, s1wyif, k1, s1wyif, k6, s2wyif, k1.

Row 27: Ssk, ktbl, p6, t3f, p6, ktbl, k2tog. 21sts

Row 28: P1, k7, s1wyif, k1, s1wyif, k7, p1.

Row 29: Ssk, k6, ktbl, k1, ktbl, k6, k2tog. 17sts

Row 30: P1, k6, s1wyif, k1, s1wyif, k6, p1.

Row 31: Ssk, k5, ktbl, k1, ktbl, k5, k2tog. 15sts

Row 32: P1, k5, s1wyif, k1, s1wyif, k5, p1.

Row 33: Ssk, k4, ktbl, k1, ktbl, k4, k2tog. 13sts

Row 34: P1, k4, s1wyif, k1, s1wyif, k4, p1.

Row 35: Ssk, k3, ktbl, k1, ktbl, k3, k2tog. 11sts

Row 36: P1, k3, s1wyif, k1, s1wyif, k3, p1.

Row 37: Ssk, k2, ktbl, k1, ktbl, k2, k2tog. 9 sts

Row 38: P1, k2, s1wyif, k1, s1wyif, k2, p1.

Row 39: Ssk, k1, ktbl, k1, ktbl, k1, k2tog. 7sts

Row 40: P1, k1, s1wyif, k1, s1wyif, k1, p1.

Row 41: Ssk, ktbl, k1, ktbl, k2tog. 5sts

Row 42: P1, s1wyif, k1, s1wyif, p1.

Row 43: Ssk, k1, k2tog. 3sts

Row 44: P1, k1, p1.

Row 45: Cdd.

Wrist Warmers

CO 21sts using cable method with smaller needles. Knit Rows 1-24 of Wrist Warmer using chart or written instructions.
Repeat Rows 7-24 two more times. Continue knitting Rows 25-60. The buttonholes are worked as k2tog on Rows 43, 49 and 55. Each of these is followed with a yo on the next row.

Wrist Warmer Chart (see opposite)

Wrist Warmer Written Instructions

Rows 1 and 3 (RS): K1, *ktbl, p1*, rep * to * 8 more times, ktbl, k1.

Rows 2 and 4 (WS): P1, s1wyif, k1, s1wyif, k1, s1wyif, k1, s1wyif, k1, s1wyif, k1, s1wyif, k1, s1wyif, k1, s1wyif, k1, s1wyif, k1, s1wyif, p1.

Row 5: K1, yo, *ktbl, p1*, rep * to * nine times, ktbl, yo, k1.

Row 6: K2, s1wyif, k7, s1wyif, k1, s1wyif, k7, s1wyif, k2.

Repeat pattern

Row 7: K1, yo, ktbl, yo2, ktbl, p7, t3f, p7, ktbl, yo2, ktbl, yo, k1.

Row 8: K2, s1wyif, p1, k1, s1wyif, k7, s1wyif, k7, s1wyif, k1, p1, s1wyif, k2.

Row 9: K2, yo, ktbl, yo, k2, ktbl, p6, t2b, p1, t2f, p6, ktbl, k2, yo, ktbl, yo, k2.

Row 10: K3, s1wyif, k3, s1wyif, k6, s1wyif, k3, s1wyif, k6, s1wyif, k3, s1wyif, k3.
Row 11: K3, yo, ktbl, yo, k3, ktbl, p5, t2b, p3, t2f, p5, ktbl, k3, yo, ktbl, yo, k3.
Row 12: K4, s1wyif, k4, s1wyif, k5, s1wyif, k5, s1wyif, k5, s1wyif, k4, s1wyif, k4.
Row 13: Ssk, k2, yo, ktbl, yo, k2, k2tog, ktbl, p4, t2b, p5, t2f, p4, ktbl, ssk, k2, yo, ktbl, yo, k2, k2tog.
Row 14: K4, s1wyif, k4, s1wyif, k4, s1wyif, k7, s1wyif, k4, s1wyif, k4, s1wyif, k4.
Row 15: Ssk, k2, ktbl, k2, k2tog, ktbl, p3, t2r, p7, t2l, p3, ktbl, ssk, k2, ktbl, k2, k2tog.
Row 16: K3, s1wyif, k3, s1wyif, k3, s2wyif, k7, s2wyif, k3, s1wyif, k3, s1wyif, k3.

if you want a more substantial piece, work the neck wrap into a scarf by knitting more repeat rows of the main pattern

Row 17: Ssk, k1, ktbl, k1, k2tog, ktbl, p2, t2b, t2f, p5, t2b, t2f, p2, ktbl, ssk, k1, ktbl, k1, k2tog.
Row 18: K2, s1wyif, k2, s1wyif, k2, s1wyif, k2, s1wyif, k5, s1wyif, k2, s1wyif, k2, s1wyif, k2.
Row 19: Ssk, ktbl, k2tog, ktbl, p1, t2b, p2, t2f, p3, t2b, p2, t2f, p1, ktbl, ssk, ktbl, k2tog.
Row 20: K1, s1wyif, k1, s1wyif, k1, s1wyif, k4, s1wyif, k3, s1wyif, k4, s1wyif, k1, s1wyif, k1, s1wyif, k1.
Row 21: Cdd, ktbl, t2b, p4, t2f, p1, t2b, p4, t2f, ktbl, cdd.
Row 22: K1, s2wyif, k6, s1wyif, k1, s1wyif, k6, s2wyif, k1.
Row 23: K1, t2r, p6, ktbl, p1, ktbl, p6, t2l, k1.
Row 24: K1, s2wyif, yo, k6, s1wyif, k1, s1wyif, k6, yo, s2wyif, k1.

Repeat Rows 7-24 two more times.

Tail End and Buttonholes
Row 25: K1, yo, ktbl, yo2, ktbl, p7, t3f, p7, ktbl, yo2, ktbl, yo, k1.
Row 26: K2, s1wyif, p1, k1, s1wyif, k7, s1wyif, k1, s1wyif, k7, s1wyif, k1, p1, s1wyif, k2.
Row 27: K2, yo, ktbl, yo, k2, ktbl, p6, t2b, p1, t2f, p6, ktbl, k2, yo, ktbl, yo, k2.

Row 28: K3, s1wyif, k3, s1wyif, k6, s1wyif, k3, s1wyif, k6, s1wyif, k3, s1wyif, k3.
Row 29: K3, yo, ktbl, yo, k3, ktbl, p5, t2b, p3, t2f, p5, ktbl, k3, yo, ktbl, yo, k3.
Row 30: K4, s1wyif, k4, s1wyif, k5, s1wyif, k5, s1wyif, k5, s1wyif, k4, s1wyif, k4.
Row 31: Ssk, k2, yo, ktbl, yo, k2, k2tog, ktbl, p4, t2b, p5, t2f, p4, ktbl, ssk, k2, yo, ktbl, yo, k2, k2tog.
Row 32: K9, s1wyif, k4, s1wyif, k7, s1wyif, k4, s1wyif, k9.
Row 33: Ssk, k2, ktbl, k2, k2tog, ktbl, p3, t2r, p7, t2l, p3, ktbl, ssk, k2, ktbl, k2, k2tog.
Row 34: K3, s1wyif, k3, s1wyif, k3, s2wyif, k7, s2wyif, k3, s1wyif, k3, s1wyif, k3.
Row 35: Ssk, k1, ktbl, k1, k2tog, ktbl, p2, t2b, t2f, p5, t2b, t2f, p2, ktbl, ssk, k1, ktbl, k1, k2tog.
Row 36: K2, s1wyif, k2, s1wyif, k2, s1wyif, k2, s1wyif, k5, s1wyif, k2, s1wyif, k2, s1wyif, k2, s1wyif, k2.
Row 37: Ssk, ktbl, k2tog, ktbl, p1, t2b, p2, t2f, p3, t2b, p2, t2f, p1, ktbl, ssk, ktbl, k2tog.
Row 38: K1, s1wyif, k1, s1wyif, k1, s1wyif, k4, s1wyif, k3, s1wyif, k4, s1wyif, k1, s1wyif, k1, s1wyif, k1.
Row 39: Cdd, ktbl, t2b, p4, t2f, p1, t2b, p4, t2f, ktbl, cdd.
Row 40: K1, s2wyif, k6, s1wyif, k1, s1wyif, k6, s2wyif, k1.
Row 41: K1, t2r, p6, t3f, p6, t2l, k1.
Row 42: P1, s2wyif, k6, s1wyif, k1, s1wyif, k6, s2wyif, p1.
Row 43: Ssk, ktbl, p6, ktbl, k2tog, p6, ktbl, k2tog.
Row 44: P1, s1wyif, k6, s1wyif, yo, s1wyif, k6, s1wyif, p1.
Row 45: Ssk, p5, ktbl, p1, ktbl, p5, k2tog.
Row 46: P1, k5, s1wyif, k1, s1wyif, k5, p1.
Row 47: Ssk, p4, t3f, p4, k2tog.
Row 48: P1, k4, s1wyif, k1, s1wyif, k4, p1.
Row 49: Ssk, p3, ktbl, k2tog, p3, k2tog.
Row 50: P1, k3, s1wyif, yo, s1wyif, k3, p1.
Row 51: Ssk, p2, ktbl, p1, ktbl, p2, k2tog.
Row 52: P1, k2, s1wyif, k1, s1wyif, k2, p1.
Row 53: Ssk, p1, t3f, p1, k2tog.
Row 54: P1, k1, s1wyif, k1, s1wyif, k1, p1.
Row 55: Ssk, ktbl, k2tog twice.
Row 56: P1, s1wyif, yo, s1wyif, p1.
Row 57: Ktbl, p1, ktbl.
Row 58: Ssp, k1, p2tog.
Row 59: K1, p1, k1.
Row 60: Cdd.

Weave in ends and gently wet block when finished. Sew buttons in corresponding places to the buttonholes.

This sweater was designed with our own wardrobes in mind. Both Susan and I like to wear layers. We wanted a cardigan that would look good on a full bust and could be worn open or closed with a variety of fasteners. We also wanted flattering lines ~ I'd love a garter yoke but those garter stitches make bulging horizontal lines in all the wrong places. The moss stitch yoke is firm and flattering, while the moss rib pinches in the waist, keeping the sweater from looking shapeless. The lace in Cinnamon Girl is more textural than open, giving just the right amount of interest.

Sizes: S (M, L)
Bust (measured flat) ~ 41cm/16in (46cm/18in, 51cm/20in)
Upper arm circumference ~ 28cm/11in (30cm/12in, 32cm/12.5in)
Distance from shoulder to underarm 26cm/10in (28cm/11in, 30cm/12in)
Skirt length (short version) ~ 25cm/10in from bottom of twisted rib, 55cm/22in overall
Skirt length (long version) ~ 35cm/14in from bottom of twisted rib, 65cm/25.5in overall
3/4 sleeve length ~ 27cm/11in
Short sleeve length ~ 10cm/4in

Note: The important fit areas are across the bust and the sleeve width at upper arm. You can follow the directions for different sizes within the same sweater. For instance, if you want to make the small size sweater but increase the upper arm circumference to the medium size, just carry on making the increases in the arm section, following the medium size. You can also stop increasing across the back width and carry on increasing across the bust or vice versa if this suits your figure shape.

Yarn:
'Pea Soup' version (opposite) with no flare, long skirt length and short sleeves:
Berroco Ultra Alpaca Light: 50% super fine alpaca, 50% Peruvian wool, 50g = 133m/144yd, 6 (7, 7) skeins
Colour shown: 4275 Pea Soup Mix

'Savannah' version (previous page) with flare, short skirt length and 3/4 sleeves:
Juno Pearl: 40% superfine alpaca, 40% merino and 20% silk, 100g = 230m/251yd, 4 (4, 5) skeins
Colour shown: Savannah

Our models are knit in two slightly different yarns. Berroco Ultra Alpaca Light is listed as a light DK yarn, while the Juno Pearl is a thick DK. They both work well but I wouldn't choose a light DK yarn with any more alpaca or silk in it; the yarn needs to have some loft. The amounts of yarn listed in the pattern are given for the styles on the models, but if you choose to vary the size, length, flare or sleeves you may need a bit more or a bit less. When buying yarn it is always better to get extra rather than not enough, especially if you choose a hand-dyed yarn.

Gauge:
10cm/4in = 18sts x 29 rows in moss stitch

Needles:
4mm/US 6 straight needles in a long length or 100cm/40in circular needles
4mm/US 6 dpns or 100cm/40in circular using 'magic loop' technique for sleeves

Notions: scrap yarn, stitch markers, stitch holders, darning needle

Notes On Construction:
Cinnamon Girl is begun by knitting the Lace-Cable that wraps around the back neckline. This Lace-Cable continues down the front openings, while stitches are picked up from the Lace-Cable Band edge for the back, fronts and sleeves. The sweater is knit down, increasing in the moss stitch areas, between the Lace-Cable Bands that edge the fronts and frame the sleeves. When the knitting is completed to the underarms, the sleeves are put on stitch holders to be picked up and finished later, while the body knitting continues. The moss stitch continues to just below the bust, where a slight tapering is given by the band of twisted moss rib stitch. The raglan Lace-Cable Bands and Lace-

I knew Cinnamon Girl should be knit from the top down. It gives the knitter so much more opportunity to achieve a good fit and is much more versatile for styling decisions ~ you can:
 • Knit until you reach the width and length you like (or have enough yarn for)
 • Knit the back width a different size than the front width (good for those with large busts and small backs)
 • Add more or less flare after the yoke
 • Have short, three-quarter or long sleeves
 • Taper hem of sleeves or let flare into a bell shape
 • Add pockets
You can customise all these details as you go along, trying on the sweater to see what suits you best.
Just make sure you get some extra yarn (a skein should do it) if you are making longer sleeves or length!

Cable front edges continue uninterrupted to the moss stitch hem. The sweater flares slightly after the twisted moss stitch as it is increased into a plain stocking stitch bottom. The hem of the sweater is finished with 3cm/1in of moss stitch. The sleeve stitches are then picked up and finished to the desired length, either with a twisted moss rib to taper them at the hem, or finished with moss stitch.

Moss Stitch:
Odd number of stitches:
Row 1: *K1, p1*, rep * to * across row.
Row 2: *K1, p1*, rep * to * across row.
Even number of stitches:
Row 1: *K1, p1*, rep * to * across row.
Row 2: *P1, k1*, rep * to * across row.

Pattern:

Neckline cable
Using scrap yarn, CO 9sts with a provisional cast on. Work Back Neckline Lace-Cable Chart or Written Instructions Rows 1-6 a total of 11 (12, 13) times. Work Rows 1-5 once more. You will now have worked 71 (77, 83) rows.

Back Neckline Lace-Cable Chart
(see following page)

Back Neckline Lace-Cable Written Instructions
Row 1 (WS): P2, ktbl, p3, ktbl twice, k1.
Row 2 (RS): S1wyif, ktbl, ptbl, yo, sk2p, yo, ptbl, k2.
Row 3: P2, ktbl, p3, ktbl twice, k1.
Row 4: S1wyif, ktbl, ptbl, k1, yo, ssk, ptbl, k2.
Row 5: P2, ktbl, p3, ktbl twice, k1.

Row 6: S1wyif, ktbl, ptbl, k3, ptbl, k2.

Yoke Set Up

Find the centre back of neckline on the k2 edge by folding in half, mark with a pin or waste yarn.

Next row: S1wyif, ktbl, ptbl, k3, ptbl, ssk, pick up 36 (39, 42)sts before the centre back marker, from the plain edge of the Lace-Cable, between the first and second edge stitches. Pick up another 37 (40, 43)sts from the remainder of the cable collar in the same way. Working from the 9sts held on the provisional cast on edge, k2tog, ptbl, k3, ptbl, ktbl, k1. 89 (95, 101)sts

Next row: S1wyif, ktbl twice, p3, ktbl, ptbl, pm, p1, pm, *ptbl, ktbl, p3, ktbl, ptbl*, pm, (p1, k1) four (five, six) times, p1, pm, rep * to *, pm, (p1, k1) twelve (thirteen, fourteen) times, p1, pm, rep * to *, pm, (p1, k1) four (five, six) times, p1, pm, rep * to *, pm, p1, pm, ptbl, ktbl, p3, k2 tbl, k1. 10st markers; 89 (95, 101)sts

The Lace-Cable Bands are counted as part of the fronts and back, not the sleeves. This is how the work divides:

Fronts: Total 16sts each; 8sts front Lace-Cable Bands, 1st in moss st, 7sts sleeve Lace-Cable Bands.

Sleeves: Total 9 (11, 13)sts each in moss st.

Back: Total 39 (41, 43)sts; 7sts right sleeve Lace-Cable Band, 25 (27, 29)sts in moss st, 7sts left sleeve Lace-Cable Band.

Increases will occur in the moss stitch sections only, next to the Lace-Cable Bands, at the stitch markers.

Work *in pattern* as follows:

Follow the chart (see below) or written instructions for the Left Front Lace-Cable Band for the first 8sts, slm, M1 if required, work moss st over the Left Front stitches, M1 if required, slm, work Lace-Cable Band, slm, M1 if required, work moss st over the sleeve, slm, M1 if required, work Lace-Cable Band, slm, M1 if required, work moss st over the Back, M1 if required, slm, work Lace-Cable Band, slm, M1 if required, work sleeve moss sts, M1 if required, slm, work Lace-Cable Band, slm, M1 if required, work front moss stitches, M1 if required, slm, work Right Front Lace-Cable Band.

Left-Front Lace-Cable Band

Row 1 (RS): S1wyif, ktbl, ptbl, yo, sk2p, yo, ptbl, ktbl.
Row 2 (WS): Ptbl, ktbl, p3, ktbl twice, k1.
Row 3: S1wyif, ktbl, ptbl, k1, yo, ssk, ptbl, ktbl.
Row 4: Ptbl, ktbl, p3, ktbl twice, k1.
Row 5: S1wyif, ktbl, ptbl, k3, ptbl, ktbl.
Row 6: Ptbl, ktbl, p3, ktbl twice, k1.

Right Front Lace-Cable Band

Row 1 (RS): Ktbl, ptbl, yo, sk2p, yo, ptbl, ktbl, k1.
Row 2 (WS): S1wyib, ktbl twice, p3, ktbl, ptbl.

Back Neckline Lace-Cable Chart

Left-Front Lace-Cable Band

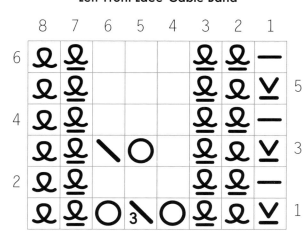

Row 3: Ktbl, ptbl, ssk, yo, k1, ptbl, ktbl, k1.
Row 4: S1wyib, ktbl twice, p3, ktbl, ptbl.
Row 5: Ktbl, ptbl, k3, ptbl, ktbl, k1.
Row 6: S1wyib, ktbl twice, p3, ktbl, ptbl.

Lace-Cable Band
Row 1 (RS): Ktbl, ptbl, yo, sk2p, yo, ptbl, ktbl.
Row 2 (WS): Ptbl, ktbl, p3, ktbl, ptbl.
Row 3: Ktbl, ptbl, k1, yo, ssk, ptbl, ktbl.
Row 4: Ptbl, ktbl, p3, ktbl, ptbl.
Row 5: Ktbl, ptbl, k3, ptbl, ktbl.
Row 6: Ptbl, ktbl, p3, ktbl, ptbl.

Where a row is not listed, there are no increases and it should be worked *in pattern*.

Row 1 (RS): M1 at each of the markers. 10sts inc; 99 (105, 111)sts
Row 3: M1 at each of the sleeve edge markers, but not at fronts. 8sts inc; 107 (113, 119)sts
Row 5: M1 at each of the sleeve edge markers, but not at fronts. 8sts inc; 115 (121, 127)sts
Row 7: M1 at each of the sleeve edge markers, but not at fronts. 8sts inc; 123 (129, 135)sts
Row 9: M1 at each of the markers. 10sts inc; 133 (139, 145)sts
Row 11: M1 at each of the sleeve edge markers, but not at fronts. 8sts inc; 141 (147, 153)sts
Row 15: M1 at each of the markers. 10sts inc; 151 (157, 163)sts
Row 19: M1 at each of the markers. 10sts inc; 161

(167, 173)sts
Row 23: M1 at each of the markers. 10sts inc; 171 (177, 183)sts
Row 27: M1 at each of the markers. 10sts inc; 181 (187, 193)sts
Row 31: M1 at each of the markers. 10sts inc; 191 (197, 203)sts
Row 35: M1 at each of the markers. 10sts inc; 201 (207, 213)sts
Row 39:
Size S: M1 at each of the sleeve edge markers, but not at fronts. 8sts inc; 209sts.
Sizes M & L: M1 at each of the markers. 10 sts inc; (217, 223)sts.
Row 43:
Sizes S & M: M1 at each of the sleeve edge markers, but not at fronts. 8sts inc; 217 (225)sts
Size L: M1 at each of the markers. 10sts inc; 233sts.
Row 47:
All sizes: M1 at each of the sleeve edge markers, but not at fronts. 8sts inc; 225 (233, 241)sts

No more increases for size S; continue to work 225sts in pattern for 13 more rows and then follow the instructions for separate sleeve stitches.

For sizes M & L only:
Row 51: M1 at each of the sleeve edge markers, but not at fronts. 8sts inc; (241, 249)sts
Row 54: M1 at each of the sleeve edge markers, but not at fronts. 8sts inc; (249, 257)sts

Right-Front Lace-Cable Band

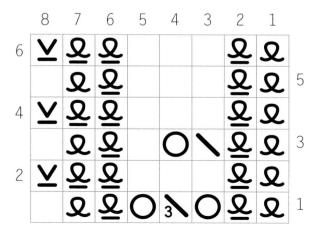

Lace Cable Band

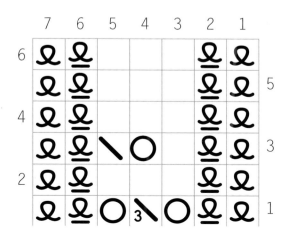

No more increases for size M; continue to work 249sts in pattern for 12 more rows and then follow the instructions for separate sleeve stitches.

For size L only:
Row 57: M1 at each of the sleeve edge markers, but not at fronts. 8sts inc; 265sts
Row 61: M1 at each of the sleeve edge markers, but not at fronts. 8sts inc; 273sts.

No more increases for size L, continue to work 273sts *in pattern* 9 more rows and then follow the instructions for separate sleeve stitches.

Divide Sleeve Stitches and Try On
Run a length of scrap yarn through the 39 (42, 45)sts of the Left Front of body. Place the 39 (45, 54) left sleeve stitches on a separate length of scrap yarn. Continue the scrap yarn from the front stitches around to pick up the 55 (61, 67) back stitches. Place the 39 (45, 54) right sleeve stitches on a third length of scrap yarn. Continue the scrap yarn from the back around to the remaining 39 (42, 45)sts of the front right of body. Tie off the lengths of yarn holding the sleeve stitches (allowing an extra 4cm/1.5in of length on each) and try on. If you are happy with the bust circumference continue on to knitting the body. If you want extra width or length at this point, you can rip back to the row where you stopped increasing and continue increasing 8sts every fourth row until you have the desired width and length.

Continue Knitting Body
Pop your needle back through the Left Front, Back and Right Front stitches, leaving the sleeves on the lengths of scrap yarn. Knit the Left Front stitches *in pattern*, up to the armhole. Using a provisional cast on, add 9sts under the arm. Continue knitting the back *in pattern* to the right underarm. Again, using a provisional cast on, add 9sts and then continue knitting front *in pattern*, working the new underarm stitches in moss stitch. 151 (163, 175)sts.

Work in pattern for another 5 rows. The yoke should now fall just below your bust line. The weight of the yarn will pull the sweater lower at this point when it is finished. Continue all the Lace-Cable Bands *in pattern*. The moss stitches now become twisted moss rib.

Set Up Row (RS):
Continue to follow the chart or written instructions for the Left Front Lace-Cable Band for the first 8sts, slm, continue row in your size as follows:

Left Front Moss Stitch:
Size S: (P1, k1) in first st, (ktbl, k1, ptbl, k1) five times, ktbl, k1, ptbl, slm. (25sts in section)
Size M: Ptbl, k2tog, (ktbl, k1, ptbl, k1) five times, ktbl, k2 tog, ptbl, slm. (25sts in section)
Size L: Ptbl, k1 , (ktbl, k1, ptbl, k1) six times, ktbl, k2tog, ptbl, slm. (29sts in section)

Continue to work Lace-Cable Band over the next 7sts, slm, *ptbl, k1, ktbl, k1*, repeat * to * until last st, ptbl over the 9 cast on underarm sts, slm.

Continue to work Lace-Cable Band over the next 7sts, slm.

Back Moss Stitch:
Size S: Ptbl, k2tog, (ktbl, k1, ptbl, k1) twelve times, ktbl, k2 tog, ptbl, slm. (53sts in section)
Size M: (Ptbl, k1, ktbl, k1), fifteen times, ptbl. (61sts in section)
Size L: Ptbl, k2tog, (ktbl, k1, ptbl, k1) fifteen times, ktbl, k2 tog, ptbl, slm. (65sts in section)

Continue to work Lace-Cable Band over the next 7sts, slm, *ptbl, k1, ktbl, k1*, rep * to * until last st, ptbl over the 9 cast on underarm sts, slm.

Continue to work Lace-Cable Band over the next 7sts, slm.

Right Front Moss Stitch:
Size S: (P1, k1) in first st, (ktbl, k1, ptbl, k1) five times, ktbl, k1, ptbl, slm. (25sts in section)
Size M: Ptbl, k2tog, (ktbl, k1, ptbl, k1) five times, ktbl, k2 tog, ptbl, slm. (25sts in section)
Size L: Ptbl, k1 , (ktbl, k1, ptbl, k1) six times, ktbl, k2tog, ptbl, slm. (29sts in section)

Continue to work Right Front Lace-Cable Band. 165 (173, 185)sts

Turn and begin working Twisted Moss Rib from Row 2. Continue for 5cm/2in, ending with a WS row.

Twisted Moss Rib Chart (see right)

Twisted Moss Rib Written Instructions
Row 1 (RS): *Ptbl, k1, ktbl, k1*, rep * to * until last st, ptbl.
Row 2 (WS): Ktbl, *k1, ptbl, k1, ktbl*, rep * to * to end.

Increasing Stitches for Body
The yoke is now finished and you are ready to increase stitches for the body. The increases listed here will make the sweater flare just slightly as in our 'Pea Soup' variation, if you wish for more flare kfb into every twisted moss rib stitch instead of every second one. This would give you a final total of 286 (302, 326)sts.

Set up stocking stitch panels as follows:
Continue to follow the chart or written instructions for the Left Front Lace-Cable Band for the first 8sts, slm, (kfb, k1) 12 (12, 13 times), kfb, slm, [38(38, 43)sts in section]

Continue to work Lace-Cable Band over the next

7sts, slm,(kfb, k1) 4 times, kfb, slm, [18sts in section]

Continue to work Lace-Cable Band over the next 7sts, slm, (kfb, k1) 26 (30, 32) times, kfb, slm. [80(92, 98)sts in this section]

Continue to work Lace-Cable Band over the next 7sts, slm,(kfb, k1) 4 times, kfb, slm, [18sts in this section]

Continue to work Lace-Cable Band over the next 7sts, slm,(kfb, k1) 12(12, 13) times, kfb, slm. [38(38, 43)sts in this section]

Continue to work Right Front Lace-Cable Band for last 8sts. 236 (248, 264)sts total

Knit *in pattern* by knitting the fronts, backs and side panels in stocking stitch with Lace-Cable inserts for desired length. The Savannah version is knit for another 22cm/9in. The Pea Soup version is knit for another 32cm/12.5in.
To prevent the front Lace-Cable Bands from growing longer than the rest of the sweater it is a good idea to insert three short rows, that leave out the Front Band stitches, before knitting the moss stitch hem. (This step is not absolutely essential if you hate knitting short rows.) If you wish to do this follow the instructions for short rows below.

Short rows
There are three short rows to be worked over the entire length of the sweater skirt. They shouldn't be done all at once, but distributed evenly – their placement doesn't have to be too precise.

Starting on a WS row, work *in pattern* until you reach the first twisted knit stitch of the left front Lace-Cable Band. Slip stitch to left needle, bring yarn forward and slip stitch back to right needle, wrapping twisted knit stitch. Work back on the RS, *in pattern,* to the first twisted purl stitch of Right

Twisted Moss Rib

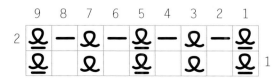

'pea soup' version using
berroco 'ultra alpaca light dk'

Front Lace-Cable Band. Slip purl stitch to the left needle, bring yarn forward and slip stitch back to right needle, wrapping twisted purl stitch.

Work back on the WS, *in pattern*, to the wrapped stitch. Lift the wrap onto the needle so that you knit the wrap together with the twisted knit stitch. Finish the row with the Front Lace-Cable Band.

Work back on the RS, *in pattern*, to the wrapped stitch. Lift the wrap onto the needle so that you purl the wrap together with the twisted purl stitch.

The front bands will now be on a different row of the Lace-Cable pattern than the other bands. Work two more short rows, evenly spaced before the moss hem so that the sweater ends with all the Lace-Cable Bands on Row 6 of pattern.

Moss Stitch Hem

Knit 3cm in moss st. Loosely cast off knitwise.

Sleeves

Pick up 39 (45, 54)sts from scrap yarn plus 9sts from underarm provisional cast on. For sizes S and M, pick up an extra stitch from underarm by kfb in order to give you an odd number of stitches total so that you can work in moss stitch. 49 (55, 63)sts

You may also pick up a couple of extra stitches next to the underarm stitches and knit them together with the yoke stitches to close any holes that may form or add extra sleeve width.

Savannah Version

Knit in moss stitch for 26cm/10in and then loosely cast off knitwise. The moss stitch will flare a little after it is worn for a while.

Pea Soup Version

Knit in moss stitch for 7cm/3in. Finish sleeve with 3cm/1in of twisted moss rib. This gives the sleeves a firm, non-flaring edge.

The twisted moss rib is made up of a 4-stitch repeat so you will need to decrease a few stitches to have a sleeve number that divides by 4. So for the **size S** you will need to decrease from 49sts to 48sts, for the **size M** you will need to increase one stitch from 55 to 56sts, and for **size L** you will need to decrease from 63 to 60sts.

Cast off sleeve stitches and weave in ends. Wet block gently to open lace bands.

bertie

Bertie is our take on a classic knitted doll. We have seen examples of this kind of folk doll with his hands in his pockets, but couldn't find any patterns for him so we made one up! The pattern is written for knitting flat and then sewing up, so that he is achievable for a beginner, however, Bertie can be knit in the round even more quickly with dpns or by using the 'magic loop' technique

Size:
Our samples range from 19cm/7.5in - 25cm/10in tall

Yarn:
Bertie can be made from leftovers of whatever yarns you have to hand. Ideally use the same weight of yarn throughout, but if you do use different thicknesses, plan so that the heavier yarns get used in the thicker areas of the body, such as his sweater or hat. I have used a selection of sock and DK weight yarns that were left over from other projects in the book. Rowan Tweed yarns or Jamieson's Shetland Spindrift would work beautifully with their wide ranges of colours and matted textures.

Gauge & Needles: You want a tight tension so that the stuffing won't sneak out. Use smaller needles for your yarn than recommended or typical.

We have used the smallest possible needle size for each yarn. For example, our Berties were made with predominantly 4 ply yarn and we knit them on 2.5mm needles. Size will vary depending on the yarn and needles used.

Notions: darning needle, stuffing

Note:
When you change colour after each section, leave a 15cm/6in tail of the old yarn and at least a 30cm/12in tail of the new yarn. You then have plenty of thread for sewing up the seams.

See our blog page for tips on knitting Bertie in the round: loopknitlounge.com

Instructions

1. CO 36sts for Bertie's shoes, and knit 6 rows in stocking stitch.

2. Change colour for Bertie's trousers. (K8, kfb) four times. 40sts
Knit one more row, so that you have a garter ridge for his cuffs.

3. Knit 16 rows in st st.
(Try striped or fairisle if you want patterned trousers.)

4. Change colour for Bertie's sweater. Knit 18 rows in st st.

5. Change colour for Bertie's face. K2tog twenty times. 20sts dec; 20sts.
Knit 10 rows.

6. Change colour for Bertie's hat. K2, *kfb, k2*, rep from * to * 5 more times. 26sts
Knit three more rows so that there are two ridges of garter stitch.

7. *K2, k2tog*, rep from * to * 5 more times, k2. 20sts
Knit 7 more rows of st st.

8. (K2, k2tog) five times. 15sts
Knit 1 more row of st st.

9. (K1, k2tog) five times. 10sts
Knit 1 more row of st st.

10. Cut yarn, leaving a 30cm/12in tail and thread on darning needle. Bring needle through all stitches twice, drawing them into a circle. Remove darning needle, but don't cut thread; you can use it for sewing later.
Follow instructions for assembly and finishing.

assembly

Always leave the end of threads hanging, don't darn them in until you are finished, as you may want to use them again.

• Fold Bertie so that the seam is centred at his back. Using the beginning of the shoe yarn, sew up the seam at the bottom of Bertie's feet.

• Sew up the back seam of his shoes and then use a running stitch in matching colour yarn to sew the indentation at the centre of Bertie's shoes.

• Switch to his trouser colour and sew up the back seam to the top of the trousers.

• Use a running stitch in matching colour yarn to sew the indentation at the centre of Bertie's trousers. The indentation ends after the 16th row of his trousers. Darn in the end of the yarn and trim.

• Stuff each of Bertie's feet and trousers up to his waist, using a pencil end to compact the stuffing and make it firm.

• Use the sweater yarn to sew up the back seam to his neck.

• To create arms, sew a running stitch channel, about 8sts wide, along each of his sides. Begin the running stitch two rows up from the beginning of his sweater colour to create the hands-in-pocket illusion. Stitch the channel for 9 rows. Darn in the end of the yarn and trim.

• Stuff each of Bertie's arms and his torso up to his neckline, again using a pencil end to compact the stuffing and make it firm.

• Now sew his head and stuff in the same way and finish sewing up his hat. Leave his hat under-stuffed so that you can bend over the top point.

• Sew a running stitch around his neck to draw it in a little. Stitch some eyes near the brim of his hat and a nose in matching skin colour.

• You can also add an embroidered mouth and knit him a scarf if you like.

snowdon blanket
...and grant scarf

Chevron stitches are great fun to knit and work well here as a baby blanket or man's scarf. Snowdon can easily be enlarged to make a cosy throw by adding extra repeats of the pattern to the length and width, or you can choose a finer, 'baby' yarn and make a smaller version. You can also make the Grant Scarf wider or longer by adding extra repeats of the pattern.

Size: 80cm/31.5in square

Yarn:
Misti Alpaca Best of Nature Chunky:
100% baby alpaca, 100g = 98m/109yd
Colour A: 3 skeins – BN03 Basil
Colour B: 2 skeins – BN05 Lilac
Colour C: 1 skein – BN01 Blue corn

Needles: 6mm/US 10, 100cm/40in circular needle

Gauge: 10cm/4in = 14sts x 20 rows in chevron stitch, after blocking
Be aware that chevron stitch grows in length and shrinks in width dramatically after it is blocked; what starts out looking like a short, wide blanket grows to the right proportions after wet blocking.

Pattern:
With Colour B, CO 115sts. Knit 6 rows (3 ridges) in garter stitch. Switch to Colour A to begin chevron pattern. Continue by following chart or written instructions.

Snowdon Blanket Written Instructions
Row 1 (RS): With Colour A, k2, *yo, k5, k3tog, k5, yo, k1*, rep * to * seven more times, k1.
Row 2 (WS): K2, purl to last 2sts, k2.
Rows 3&4: Knit all stitches.

Snowden Blanket Chart

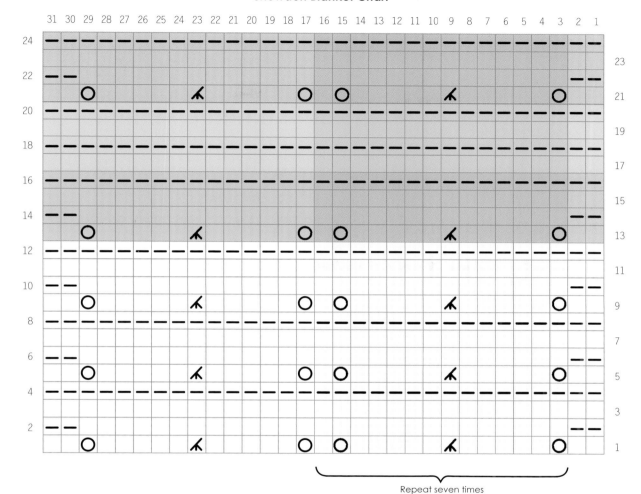

Repeat seven times

Rows 5-12: Rep rows 1-4 twice more in Colour A.
Row 13 (RS): With Colour B, k2, *yo, k5, k3tog, k5, yo, k1*, rep * to * seven more times, k1.
Row 14 (WS): K2, purl to last 2sts, k2.
Rows 15&16: Knit all stitches.
Rows 17-20: With Colour C, knit all stitches.
Rows 21-24: With Colour B, rep rows 13-16.

These 24 rows of the chart or written instructions make up the repeat pattern of the blanket. Repeat the 24 row sequence five more times.

Make a final repeat of Rows 1-12 in Colour A and then knit 6 rows (3 ridges) of Colour B in garter stitch. Cast off knitwise and weave in all ends.

Blocking
The stitch proportions will change radically when wet blocked. Wash blanket and wrap in a towel to remove excess water. Lay flat on a fresh towel to dry, stretching lengthwise, to fit dimensions and pointing ends of chevrons. There is no need to pin in position, just leave to dry flat.

...and grant scarf

Size: length - 200cm/79in, width - 22cm/9in

Yarn:
Misti Alpaca Chunky and Chunky Handpaints:
100% baby alpaca, 100g = 98m/109yd
Colour A: 2 skeins - 716 Blue Lake
Colour B: 1 skein - CP27 Falstaff
Colour C: 1 skein - 410 Natural Brown

Needles: 6mm/US 10 straight or circular needles

Gauge: 10cm/4in = 14sts x 20 rows in chevron stitch, after blocking (see Snowdon gauge information on previous page)

Pattern:
Cast on 33sts in Colour C and knit 6 rows (3 ridges) in garter stitch. Follow chart or written instructions for scarf.

Written Instructions for Grant Scarf
Row 1 (RS): With Colour A, k2, k2tog, *k5, yo, k1, yo, k5,* k3tog, rep * to * once more, ssk, k2.
Row 2 (WS): K2, p29, k2.
Rows 3&4: Knit all stitches.
Rows 5-12: Rep rows 1-4 twice more.
Row 13 (RS): With Colour B, k2, k2tog, *k5, yo, k1, yo, k5,* k3tog, rep * to * once more, ssk, k2.
Row 14: K2, p29, k2.
Rows 15&16: Knit all stitches.

Rows 17-20: With Colour C, knit all stitches.
Rows 21-24: With Colour B, rep rows 13-16.

These 24 rows of chart or written instructions make up the repeat pattern of the scarf. Repeat the sequence twelve times. Make a final repeat of Rows 1-12 with Colour A and then knit 6 rows (3 ridges) with Colour C in garter stitch. Cast off knitwise and weave in ends.

Blocking
Block as suggested on previous page for Snowdon Blanket.

Grant Scarf Chart

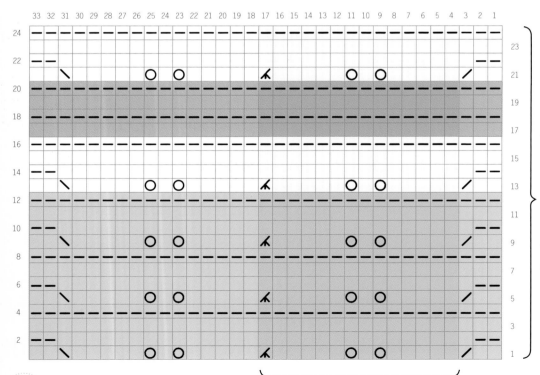

Repeat row sequence twelve and a half times

The repeat sequence

88

owl cowls, crow waltzes
and other patterns from our blog

owl cowl shown here knit with quince & co 'puffin' in peacock
with horn toggles. we often post free patterns on our blog, designed by
juju ~ here is a selection of some of them; the owl cowl, layering shrug
and crow waltz shawl ~ please feel free to download them at
www.loopknitlounge.com

above: layering shrug knit in old maiden aunt 'alpaca silk sport/fine dk' in bitterbug
opposite: pile of hand knit shrugs and shawls. see page ninety~nine for details of patterns and yarns used

crow waltz shawl

shown here knit with
old maiden aunt
'sportweight/fine dk' in
strange rock n' rollers
and gothic. opposite: detail
of crow waltz shawl
knit with madelinetosh
'pashmina' in windowpane
and silver fox

pictured here:
lantern moon rosewood
needles and
madelinetosh yarn
opposite: twigs
wrapped in juno 'alice'
in selection of plums
and mauve colours

in case you were wondering...

Cover: Yarns wound on sticks are a selection of Juno 'Alice'.

Inside front page and page 1: Handmade ceramic owl by Nathalie Lete at Loop; yarn wound on sticks, as on cover.
Shawls from left: Layering Shrug knit in Old Maiden Aunt in Bitterbug, Crow Waltz Shawl knit in madelinetosh Pashmina in Silver Fox and Windowpane, Crow Waltz Shawl knit in Old Maiden Aunt in Gothic and Strange Rock n' Rollers, Prairie Shawl knit in Malabrigo Lace in Frank Ochre and Berry Wrap knit in bc garn Lucca Tweed.
Handmade wooden board with ceramic hooks from Buddug Humphreys & Jessie Chorley, Columbia Road, London.

Contents page: One of a kind Julie Arkell doll from a selection at Loop.

Page 6/7: Yarns are a selection of Old Maiden Aunt.

Page 40: Sajou haberdashery, Nathalie Lete silkscreen prints, Julie Arkell dolls and vintage ribbons and haberdashery. The crochet blanket on the chair is the Babette Blanket by Kathryn Merrick (see kathrynmerrick.com or interweavestore.com).

Page 68/69: Selection of vintage ribbons and buttons with madelinetosh Vintage in Olivia.

Page 73: Handpainted wallpaper on our wall made by Nama Rococo (namarococo.com).

Page 93: On chair from top: Crow Waltz Shawl (blues) in madelinetosh Pashmina in Windowpane and Silver Fox, Layering Shrug (green) as before on page 92, Layering Shrug (mauves) knit with DyeForYarn Fingering Merino & Silk in Losing the Dark Dream, just seen; Prairie Shawl in madelinetosh Prairie in Fragrant.
On the bottom is the Eliina Shawl by Lankakomero (lovely free pattern on ravelry.com) knit in Socks That Rock in Mochaberry.

Page 94: Brooch is made from an oval carved bone bird button with a clasp put on as backing.

Page 97: Nathalie Lete handmade ceramic owl and Juno Alice yarns.

Page 98: Oil painting bag is from Leslie Oschmann, Swarm.

This page: madelinetosh Sock in Fragrant.

heartfelt thank yous......

Loop is a textile house of treasure based in London, England. Created by Susan Cropper in 2005, it has won numerous awards for being one of the best shops in London. Stocking gorgeous knitting supplies sourced from all over the world including exquisite yarns, vintage buttons, ribbons, haberdashery, quirky handmade and vintage objects, patterns and books as well as hosting a huge range of knitting & crochet workshops and wonderful staff who are passionate about knitting.

Susan, originally from New York, has lived in London the past 24 years with her three children and is a textile junkie. When she's not busy sourcing more gorgeous stuff for Loop (or knitting), she can be found out and about at vintage markets.

Juju Vail, co-conspirator in this book, joined Loop's group of girls extraordinaire in 2009. The chatty one in the shop, Juju teaches many of the classes at Loop, hails from Canada and has lived in London for over 20 years with her husband and two children. Her gorgeous designs are often seen on Loop's blog, loopknitlounge. Juju just might be the fastest knitter in the universe.

Photographer: Kristin Perers (kristinperers.com)
All patterns designed by: Juju Vail and Susan Cropper
All drawings: Juju Vail
Styling and book design: Susan Cropper
Technical Editor: Meghan Fernandes

thank you to:
Kristin Perers, our incredible photographer.

Rachel Atkinson, our dream test knitter, mean baker and very lovely friend.
More thanks go to our other great sample knitters; Lydia Gluck, Liz Baltesz, Jemima Bicknell, Meghan Fernandes and Feline Wowretzko.

Thank you to our lovely models: Meghan Fernandes, Alice Palmer-Brown and Nichollette Yardley-Moore. And to Joy Hockman-Silverberg, my 'second mom' who flew across the ocean to help out in any way she could.

Emerald Mosley for the knitting charts.

Huge thanks to The Elk in The Woods (the-elk-in-the-woods.co.uk), and, in particular, their wonderful manager Grant, for letting us shoot in their beautiful (and our favourite!) cafe. Their delicious food can be found at 39 Camden Passage, Islington, London N1

Buddug Humphreys & Jessie Chorley for handmade paper chandelier (jandbtheshop.com)
Emily Chalmers of Caravan (caravanstyle.com) for the bird cages.

Wild Swans (wild-swans.com) and Susy Harper (susyharper.co.uk) for the loan of their very beautiful clothes for this book.

And a double thank you to Erik Youngren, a total stranger across the pond who not only once, but twice, has saved our book with his technical wizardry.

Copyright agreement

Errata

For corrections to mistakes, that we might have missed before we went to print, we offer sincere apologies.
Please see our blog, loopknitlounge.com, where corrections will be posted.

Loop is on the wonderfully eccentric Camden Passage in Islington, near Angel tube station.
Loop, 15 Camden Passage, Islington, London N1 8EA 00 44 (0) 207 288 1160
We have a beautiful online shop at www.loopknitting.com and ship all over the world.

loop

gorgeous knitting supplies

15 Camden Passage
Islington, London N1 8EA
020 7288 1160

www.loopknitting.com

special terms

backward loop A method of casting on or increasing stitches by making a loop around your left thumb and knitting a stitch in the back of the loop.

cable cast on Insert right needle between the first 2sts on left needle, wrap yarn around needle as if to knit, draw yarn through and place new loop on left needle.

cast off Also known as 'bind off'.

garter stitch Created by knitting all rows if working flat, or alternating knit and purl rows if working in the round.

knitted cast on Insert right needle into 1st st on left needle as if to knit, wrap yarn around needle as if to knit, draw yarn through and place new loop on left needle.

knitwise Stitches are mounted on needle as if to knit.

magic loop A method of knitting small circumferences in the round using one long circular needle.

provisional cast on provisional cast on: Also known as 'invisible' or 'temporary' cast on. This method of casting on uses a length of waste yarn that is removed later to reveal "live" stitches, which are then placed back on the needle and knit in the opposite direction. Can be made with two needles or with crochet method.

purlwise Stitches are mounted on needles as if to purl.

stocking stitch Also known as 'stockinette' stitch, created by alternating knit and purl rows if working flat, or knitting all rows if working in the round.